D1498469

"I met Fred several years ago in a VIP area at a Nashville venue. Unbeknownst to either of us, a few years later he would be appearing with Big & Rich as the opening act for two Bon Jovi shows in New Jersey. I hope this book inspires you as much as it and he inspire me!"

—Richie Sambora, Bon Jovi guitarist, rock star

"Every time I see Fred he tells me a new crazy story. I had no idea of the life he's lived and I can see why he has his own book!"

—Darius Rucker, award-winning country music star and lead singer of Hootie & the Blowfish

"I was touched to learn in his book that my music got Fred through a hard time in his life. Since I've known Fred, he has a smile that I am always happy to see!"

—Jewel, Grammy-nominated recording artist

"Fred is an awesome American character and I can't wait to read more of his story in his book. He has accomplished many feats that people would say are impossible. I'm a believer."

—Zac Brown, lead singer of the Zac Brown Band

TWO FOOT FRED

How
My Life Has
Come Full
Circle

FRED GILL
WITH LISA WYSOCKY

HOWARD BOOKS
A Division of Simon & Schuster, Inc.

NEW YORK NASHVILLE LONDON TORONTO SYDNEY NEW DELHI

Howard Books
A Division of Simon & Schuster, Inc.
1230 Avenue of the Americas
New York, NY 10020

First Howard Books hardcover edition June 2012

HOWARD and colophon are trademarks of Simon & Schuster, Inc.

For information about special discounts for bulk purchases, please contact Simon & Schuster Special Sales at 1-866-506-1949 or business@simonandschuster.com.

The Simon & Schuster Speakers Bureau can bring authors to your live event. For more information or to book an event, contact the Simon & Schuster Speakers Bureau at 1-866-248-3049 or visit our website at www.simonspeakers.com.

Designed by Jaime Putorti

Manufactured in the United States of America

10   9   8   7   6   5   4   3   2   1

Library of Congress Cataloging-in-Publication Data
Gill, Fred
Two Foot Fred / Fred Gill aka Two Foot Fred ; with Lisa Wysocky.
    p. cm.
1. Gill, Fred, 1974– 2. Dwarves—United States—Biography. I. Wysocky, Lisa, 1957– II. Title.
CT9992.G55A3 2012
362.196'470092—dc23
[B]
                                2011041926

ISBN 978-1-4516-3621-5
ISBN 978-1-4516-3627-7 (ebook)

For two people who are in heaven
and two people who are on earth:

Jesus and Mom, Dad and Toby

CONTENTS

FOREWORD

BY DAVE RAMSEY

A while back, I was teaching my EntreLeadership workshop to a group of powerful, hard-charging business leaders when the sound of a gravelly voice and the hum of an electric motor coming my way got my attention. I heard someone shouting, "Hey, Dave! Hey, Dave!" behind me, and that little motor was getting louder. I turned around to see a thirty-eight-inch-tall guy barreling toward me on a scooter, going a little too fast for my comfort. That was the first time I met Fred Gill, and he's been going a little too fast every time I've seen him since. I've come to learn that's just how "Two Foot" lives his life.

You know that kid in third grade who always had the answer, always had his hand up, and was always yelling, "Oh! Oh! Pick me! Pick me!" Yeah, that's Fred. He has one of the most passionate, inquisitive personalities I've ever been around—and his enthusiasm is infectious. Fred lives life *large*. He doesn't settle for a small, wimpy life; he has always set his sights on enormous goals and, somehow, he keeps knocking them out.

A lot of people work hard to cover up or lie about the challenges they face in life, but not Fred. Hey, if you're going to call yourself "Two Foot Fred," you're pretty much owning and accepting every inch of who you are! I love that about him. Seeing how he just attacks life—from huge business deals to the simple, mundane physical tasks I take for granted—inspires me. As you read this book and get to know my friend, you'll be inspired, too. You'll get a boost from a man named Two Foot, and he'll lift you up to places you couldn't reach on your own.

Just watch out for that scooter.

Dave Ramsey
New York Times bestselling author and nationally syndicated radio talk show host

INTRODUCTION

When you are three feet two inches tall, navigating the world is a constant challenge. Average-sized people take for granted many everyday things, such as getting dressed, using the bathroom, and shopping for groceries. But each of those activities can be very difficult—if not impossible—for people with dwarfism. My short stature, extremely short arms and legs, very short fingers with fused knuckles, trouble balancing, and stiff joints make even the simplest tasks utterly complicated. Despite the difficulties, however, my size and experiences have allowed me to gain a unique perspective on life. And what a life it has been and continues to be.

I was born a diastrophic dwarf and realized at a young age that my body was not like that of my parents, or any of the other people I saw in my hometown of Seymour, Indiana. But while my body was different, my mind was—and is—the same as everyone else's. I have similar thoughts, needs, and desires as most people: to get a good education, become a productive member of society, get married, and have a little (no pun intended) fun—okay, a lot of fun.

I've already gained a lifetime of experiences and have both achieved and failed at most of my goals. As long as my successes outweigh my failures, and they do, I feel I am in good shape. The last piece of my life puzzle is the marrying part, and I am working on that. In fact, my soul mate could be reading this book right now. Is it you?

When people look at me I know they see a character of sorts, a guy with a bigger-than-life smile and very short arms and legs driving a three-wheeled scooter faster than he should. I am sure most people don't get past the initial thought of, "*Wow,* it must suck to be him." But if they spent five minutes with me, they'd learn I am a friendly guy with a degree from the prestigious Ball State University Entrepreneurship Program. They'd find that I am a serial entrepreneur and own, or have owned, businesses that range from bars to mobile marketing to residential rental properties.

People might also recognize me as the funny, pint-size "pimp-dressed" guy who dances onstage with country duo Big & Rich. Or they might realize they have seen one of the music videos or movies I have been in. And if they stopped to talk for more than three seconds, they'd realize they just made a new friend, a solid friend—a friend for life and beyond.

Now for the fun part. How did a diastrophic dwarf from Seymour, Indiana, receive an education and become an author, inventor, actor, business owner, entertainer, and television personality? How did I get my driver's license when I have trouble reaching a steering wheel in a regular car, become a real estate broker when it is difficult for me to grip a pencil, and become an independent jet-setting traveler when I sometimes can't fit my scooter into a bathroom? How do I live in my own apartment by myself when I can't reach the doorknob? And how in the world did I become good friends with celebrities and other household names?

Along with unmatched determination and persistence, it took a lot of help from God, family, and great friends. I am also the consummate dot connector, networker, and lover of life, and I believe that size is merely perception. It is beyond ironic that I wound up living many of the same stories in real life that my best friend, country music superstar John Rich, pens in many of his lyrics. Country music is a genre noted for tragic tales, lost loves, hilarious story lines, and characters with true grit, and those things also are a big part of my life story. Along the way I've learned a lot (oftentimes the hard way), loved a lot, lost a lot, and am having far more than my share of fun.

Stick with me for the next couple hundred pages and you will see just how my life has truly come full circle.

Freddie Gill
(a.k.a. Fred Gill, Two Foot
Fred, Friend to All)
August 2011

1

ADAPTING TO
LIFE WITH ME

"Cut," screamed David Hogan in his British accent. "Let's effing do it again."

The rocking music was cued and the scene began to swell once again, filling the air around me.

"Three, two, one, action," called Hogan, and I began to dance like I'd never danced before.

It was April 14, 2004. I remember the date clearly, because it was the day before tax day. Through a very odd set of circumstances, I found myself dancing in a music video on a pedestrian footbridge that spanned the Cumberland River in Nashville, Tennessee. David Hogan is a veteran industry director and I was trying extremely hard to give him, and John Rich, a longtime friend and one half of the duo Big & Rich, exactly what they wanted.

At the wrap party that night, I learned that Hogan was skeptical about having me in the video and had worked me that much harder during the day. But he and everyone else ended up being pleased with my performance. I was very excited, as this was my first real experience in the entertainment business. In fact, it was my first encounter with country music beyond being a fan.

The video being shot was for a song called "Save a Horse (Ride a Cowboy)," by Big & Rich. The song and video went on to become their first big hit and established them—and me—firmly in the hearts of millions of fans worldwide. On this day, however, none of us knew we were making history.

The day before, I had driven from my hometown of Seymour, Indiana, in my blue and white 1989 converted van. The conversions were needed because, as a diastrophic dwarf, I stand three feet two inches tall. Before it was converted, my arms and legs would not have been nearly long enough to reach the pedals, steering wheel, or controls, but the conversion allowed me to travel thousands of miles up and down the road to manage my many businesses and my life.

When I arrived in Nashville I got out of the van through automatic doors that opened to allow a hydraulic lift to lower my Rascal electric scooter to the ground. Then I promptly checked into the Renaissance Hotel. I went out to dinner by myself, then set my alarm for three thirty A.M. and went to bed very early.

The next morning I was nervous, anxious, and excited all at the same time. Part of my anxiety came from not knowing what was going to happen. I felt out on a limb, as if I was jumping off a bridge without a safety net. Questions such as "Where will I use the bathroom?" and "Who will help me into my wardrobe?" rushed through my mind. These were questions that followed me every day of my life, questions that most people do not have to deal with.

I drove my scooter several blocks through the deserted early morning streets of Music City and arrived at the pedestrian footbridge a few minutes ahead of my four thirty A.M. call time. I quickly found out what a "call time" was, and about the concept of "hurry up and wait."

You couldn't miss the location; tents and floodlights were set up, and the smells of hot coffee and doughnuts were overpowering. At that time of the morning it was extremely cold, so I got a cup of coffee, introduced myself to the crew, and met some of my fellow cast members. The first person I met on set was Sarah Darling, now a rising star, who played the part of the mannequin.

Up to that point, the only person involved with the shoot that I knew was John Rich. John is the former colead singer and bass player for the band Lonestar. He also had a budding solo career. We'd met years earlier at Fan Fair (now called the CMA Music Festival). This event was, and still is, country music's premier annual fan gathering, and there, John and I had become friends.

When John hooked up with his friend Kenny Alphin, whom people call Big Kenny, they formed the duo Big & Rich. In late winter earlier that year I had gotten an unexpected and thrilling e-mail from John. He asked if I could appear in their first music video. Could I? Let me think . . . I believe my exact reply was, "When and where?"

I had to rearrange my schedule to make the shoot. This was difficult because the date kept changing. The day the shoot was finally set in stone happened to be the same day there was an open call in Alabama with the QVC network. I had intended to pitch my fledgling spice and seasonings product, Phat Freddie's, there. But I knew in my gut that appearing in this video was the opportunity of a lifetime. I didn't want to miss it.

Instead of going to Alabama, I endured both freezing-cold and blisteringly hot temperatures, long waits, and a chaotic swarm of people—and I loved every second of it. At the final wrap party, which was held at Fontanel, the former home of the legendary Barbara Mandrell and now one of Nashville's public landmarks, I had the opportunity to spend more time with John and Big Kenny, and also with their friend the then-up-and-coming country star Gretchen Wilson. I also hung out with Cowboy Troy, James Otto, and the rest of the MuzikMafia, a modern-day group of singers, artists, and musicians who pushed country music's boundaries to its limits. It was all quite a thrill.

When I look back, even I have to admit that the circumstances that brought it all together were both amazing and divine.

■　■　■

I WAS BORN July 27, 1974, the first child of Steve and Janet Gill. My dad worked third shift for a company called Cummins, in their plant that made diesel engines. During the day Dad had a dump truck and backhoe that he used in his excavating company. My mom was a first-grade schoolteacher and taught for nine years before I was born. There were no ultrasounds back then so until I was delivered, no one knew that I was a dwarf. As you can imagine, my arrival was surprising and caused quite a bit of confusion. But as you'll read, my family adapted quite readily to this unexpected transition in their life.

Along with being a dwarf, I had a cleft palate, clubfeet, scoliosis, and, as is common to diastrophic dwarves, shortened fingers and limbs, and cauliflower ears. To top it off, I was the first dwarf that our family doctor, Bill Blaisedell, had ever assisted into the world.

Back then Schneck Memorial Hospital in Seymour, Indiana, did not have the capability to handle a newborn with my medical needs, which were not fully known at the time of my birth. While my mom stayed in Seymour at the hospital, I was rushed to Riley Children's Hospital in Indianapolis, more than an hour's ambulance ride north. A caring nurse rode with me, and Riley was where I spent my first several weeks. I know my mom was worried sick about me, and not being able to be at my side during my first few days had to have been terrible for her.

Dr. Blaisedell once said in an interview for a video documentary that I produced that he had a lot of concerns about me from the moment I was born. "From the very get-go, it was obvious there would be very big health problems with Fred," he said, "but I have to give credit to his parents because they both jumped right in and did whatever they had to do to give Fred everything he needed to have a shot at doing something with his life." As of this writing, this documentary has yet to be released.

And I do have some amazing parents. In fact, my whole family was, and is, pretty remarkable. After I was born, my mom quit teaching so she could stay home to take care of me and also keep the books for my dad's businesses. It worked out well, because I had special challenges and it was best for me that she was there.

Now, as an adult, I realize that Mom was quite overprotective of me, but she was also an adaptable person who put others first. She once told me that the one thing she wanted more than anything else in life was to be a mother, so adapting her plans to benefit me was natural for her. Do unto others. It's one of God's commandments, but many of us struggle with it. Fortunately for me, although Mom was not perfect, she didn't have that particular problem.

By all accounts I was a very happy baby, but caring for any young child can be exhausting, much less a dwarf child who has multiple health problems. Giving my mom a break, Dad often took me with him as he worked hauling gravel or sand in his old, loud dump truck. I'd sit on the seat beside him and smile as he moved dirt and rock from one side of town to the other. My dad has said that this is one of his favorite memories of me, and I know the experience helped us bond when I was still very young.

As for my mom, her earliest remembrance of me was my smile. Apparently it was always there. "When Fred went home from Riley one of their resident doctors said he had never seen a baby at that age with such a big smile," she once said. "And that is Fred. He always had a smile on his face and his eyes wide open as if he were saying, 'I'm ready to take on the world.'"

But it took more than smiles and dump trucks to get me through my first few years. My cleft palate surgery and a series of surgeries on my feet kept Mom and Dad very busy. Fortunately, my parents had a lot of family and friends who could help. Everyone switched gears and pitched in, and I mean everyone. Both sets of grandparents were frequent visitors in our home, as were my aunts, uncles, and cousins. And that was good because when I was recovering from these surgeries, there was the real possibility of complications setting in quickly.

Diastrophic dwarfism is one of the most complicated types of dwarfism because it alters the body's cartilage, which in turn alters the bone structure of the body. On top of that, because the body is misshapen, colds can quickly turn into more severe respiratory problems, such as pneumonia and the inability to breathe. Mom made sure there was plenty of help on hand because she knew if she got so worn out that she too got sick, she would not be in a position to help me.

Sometimes it's hard to ask for help, but the old saying "Many hands make light work" is very true. I'm happy to say that eight of those hands belonged to my grandparents.

My grandpa John Gill worked for Dr Pepper during the time when trucks still carried glass bottles on the side of the vehicle. He later bought a little grocery store on Elm Street right there in Seymour and ran the meat counter. With a family of six, the ends and pieces of meat that he brought home came in very handy. My dad was the oldest of John Gill's four kids, and I remember his telling me that Grandpa Gill's store was the first one in Seymour, Indiana, to get approval for carry-out beer. That was a big thing back then, and a little controversial. Grandpa used to put beer that local preachers purchased in empty Wheaties boxes so members of their congregation would not see their spiritual leaders buying beer.

Grandpa sold the store in 1965. It was in the nick of time because just after that supermarkets became popular in our area. He spent his retirement years driving a school bus, and working for my dad and my uncle Ted in their various businesses. Grandpa wouldn't accept any payment, so my dad and uncle finally pitched in together and bought Grandma and him a trip to Hawaii that they enjoyed immensely.

Grandma Gill, Doris Fox Gill, worked at the store quite a bit and was a homemaker who took care of Grandpa for seven years after he had a stroke. As of the writing of this book, she is my only grandparent still alive. She remains very sharp well into her nineties, and I hope someday that I have a marriage that is as strong as Grandma and Grandpa Gill's was.

On my mom's side, my grandpa Wilson, Earl Wilson, was the first in his family to go to college. He had to leave college early, though, because his dad passed away and he had to go back home to take care of the farm. Back then, that's what you did. He later opened Earl Wilson's Garage, a service station that also wholesaled and retailed Goodyear tires, as well as Lawn-Boy mowers and related equipment.

When he retired, he and my grandma Dorothy Rueff Wilson turned the acre his warehouse was on into a woodshop and a garden. Grandma Wilson canned about a million things. I can still taste her corn, pickled okra, cucumbers, tomatoes, and my favorite, pickled Brussels sprouts. Grandma and Grandpa gave all the produce and canned goods away. That's just the kind of people they were. They were married for sixty-seven years. Another great marriage.

Grandma Wilson had a great sense of humor but was also an incessant worrier, so I know where my mom got that. She loved what I call "old lady" jewelry and amazingly ugly sweaters, and was the original great American housewife.

I mention all of this because I really do come from people who were, and are, the salt of the earth. They were always ready to help a friend, neighbor, or family member. Their values and integrity are very much a part of me, and while I have often strayed from this path, the rock-solid foundation they provided has allowed me to come full circle.

■ ■ ■

WHEN I WAS about a year old, my dad began building the house that I grew up in and where he still lives. The lot in the rural subdivision was on a low piece of ground, but Dad took his dump truck and filled in the property. He said he had drainage in mind when he dumped load after load of dirt on the land. As I grew older, I had a lot of fun sliding down that hill in the winter.

The neighborhood Mom and Dad chose was ideal for raising a family. The streets were laid out like the letter P with a horizontal line through the middle of the upper part of the letter. There was only one road that led in and out of the subdivision. Our brick ranch-style house was located on one of the outer edges of the then-growing area. The neighborhood was filling with young families and it was as safe as a place could be; it still is. If you can imagine a *Leave It to Beaver*–type neighborhood where everyone knew everyone else and kids were running in and out of neighbors' homes, that's where I grew up. I so appreciate that small-town upbringing. Plus it taught me that saying a simple please and thank-you can go a long way.

There were nineteen thousand people living in Seymour in 2010. I imagine the population was half that in the seventies, so even outside of our rural neighborhood the town was small enough that no one was a stranger. So when I was born, word spread quickly that Steve and Janet Gill's new baby was a dwarf.

There was one other dwarf child in Seymour when I was born, Jana Emkes, who was the youngest of eight children. Jana's type of dwarfism was achondroplasia, which in addition to short stature usually means the person has a curvature of the spine, bowed legs, and decreased muscle tone—as well as other symptoms.

As soon as the Emkeses heard about me, they immediately reached out to my parents. The Emkeses introduced my family to the Little People of America (LPA) organization, a nonprofit that provides support and information to people of short stature and to their families. LPA was a lifesaver for Mom and Dad. We were members of the Little Hoosiers chapter and attended monthly meetings at the homes of various members. I attended my first meeting when I was still a baby and have gone to many more meetings and conferences since then. Being able to see and interact with other child and adult dwarves let me know early on that little people were just the same as average-sized people, except their bodies were smaller. Knowing that I was not the only person in the world in a little body was awesome.

When I was born, because of my cleft palate they sewed my tongue to my bottom lip to keep me from swallowing it. My mom later jokingly said she wished they'd kept it that way because then maybe I wouldn't have talked so much.

As soon as I got to Riley, it was determined that I would have to be fed with a feeding tube for the first year of my life to allow me to develop enough to withstand the cleft palate surgery. The residents there taught Mom how to do this, but friends and family tell me now that they were afraid to feed me, so during that first year, I never left Mom's side. When I was about a year old, I had surgery to reconstruct the roof of my mouth.

Unbeknownst to me, the surgeon, Dr. Ponser, did beyond a fabulous job. When I got into the entertainment business I had my vocal cords scoped at Vanderbilt, which is a teaching hospital in Nashville. Looking inside my mouth, Vanderbilt doctors and residents could not believe I had ever had a cleft palate. The only residual effect of the cleft palate was that I had to take speech classes from kindergarten through sixth grade with Miss Dominick, a very patient and qualified pediatric speech therapist.

As I became older I hit many "normal" milestones such as rolling over and talking, but because I had clubfeet, which is a condition that causes the foot to rotate sideways, I couldn't walk until much later. It's probably a good thing, because if I had walked on schedule I would have been walking on the outsides of my ankles.

From my first year until my eighteenth, I had yearly visits with doctors at Riley. When I was three it was determined that it was time for me to have surgery to correct my clubfeet. Up to this time I had been sleeping in corrective shoes and was unable to walk. My parents were scared to death at the thought of the operation. Many dwarves have breathing problems and my parents were concerned that the anesthesia combined with the trauma of the surgery would cause respiratory failure. Over the years, Dr. Blaisedell had become a friend of the family, as he did with most of his patients. He assured my parents that I would be well taken care of.

I may have been well taken care of, but even though I was

only three, memories of the ordeal remain with me today. Nowadays, children's hospitals are light, cheerful places with carpeting, toys, and televisions. Not so in the seventies. Back then, Riley Children's Hospital was a dark, institutional place with metal doors, bars on the windows, and walls painted puke green. And the sounds. The shrieking and moaning and groaning made it sound like an insane asylum. From what I can remember, it wasn't the least bit kid-friendly.

While I had been to Riley annually for checkups, this was the first time I was old enough to remember the place and the feelings it created. I recall that my room, which I shared with another patient, was sterile and smelled of medicine and disinfectant. Just before my surgery, I was situated in the pre-op room with my parents. A huge male orderly who happened to be black came to take me to the operating room. I am the least prejudiced person on the planet but I had not been around a lot of black men of his tall stature in my three short years. In fact, the number was zero. I can't tell you how terrified I was by his color, immense size, and deep voice. But, looking back, he was kind and gentle.

To make matters worse, instead of putting me on a cart and wheeling me into the operating room, the orderly took me from my parents and carried me away in his arms. I am sure he did that as a comforting gesture, but at the time it only made the situation more frightening. I frantically looked to my parents for help, but their worried faces did nothing to relieve my growing fears. Because I was in this strange, noisy, smelly, dark place and in the arms of a total stranger, I looked to my warm and loving parents to help. I was too young to understand that through the surgery they were giving me exactly what I needed—a chance at the most "normal" life I could have.

All children look to their parents for guidance, care, and support. This is especially true for children with unique challenges. There are so many things you cannot do for yourself at that age that your bond with your caregivers—your parents—becomes that much stronger. All I knew was that I was in a very scary place, and a man who completely frightened me was taking me away from all that I knew and loved. I was about as anxiety-ridden as a child could possibly be before undergoing a major operation.

Fortunately, the surgery was successful and much of my recovery is a blur. What I do remember are the reassuring faces of my parents and grandparents, who stood around my strange-smelling metal hospital bed. My mom liked to tell the story that when I woke up, the first thing I asked for was a Coke. Later, I remember wearing heavy plaster casts and how much they hurt. When the casts were removed we found that the intern who put them on had done one of them wrong and the skin on my left foot had rubbed down to the bone. I still have that scar today.

I also distinctly remember the sound and smell of the saw when the casts were cut off. They used a buzz saw, and again, I was beyond frightened. My heart was thumping and I was shaking, even though I knew I had to remain still. One tiny move and my feet would be history. My young mind really hoped this guy knew what he was doing. He did.

Throughout the surgery and recovery, even though I was not feeling well and was often in pain, I felt warm and comforted because I knew without a doubt that I was safe.

2

TWO DWARVES ARE BETTER THAN ONE

I learned a big lesson early on in life from one of my favorite cartoon shows, *G.I. Joe*. A character on the show said, "Knowing is half the battle." So that you can also know and appreciate more about the differences in my body and my daily challenges, I will tell you more about my dwarfism.

First, other than the fact that I am obviously short, dwarfism is a general term that covers a large number of medical conditions. According to the National Institutes of Health, the term is applied to people who are, or will grow to be, less than fifty-eight inches tall. I'd say that my thirty-eight inches of height absolutely qualifies me as a dwarf.

Dwarfism is also more common than you might think. It is found in about one in twenty-five thousand people across the United States and Europe. This means that about one in twenty-five hundred people have a dwarf in their extended family and that an estimated one in every three to five hundred people in the United States personally knows someone with dwarfism. With the publication of this book, that number will change, because you and I are now officially friends.

There are many types of dwarfism, and while it is not a disability in itself, many aspects of it, such as my tight joints, fused knuckles, difficulty walking long distances, and size, can make day-to-day living a challenge. For example, in addition to doorknobs, on my own I can't reach a light switch or a sink, most of the shelves in a refrigerator, or the shelving or closet hangers found in most homes. Gripping things with my hands is also a challenge, as is washing dishes. Because I cannot reach the sink I eat off of paper plates. As I've mentioned, the type of dwarfism I have is diastrophic dysplasia. It occurs in about one in every one hundred ten thousand births and is far less common than many other types of dwarfism. That means I am one of roughly twenty-seven hundred diastrophic dwarves in the world. Remember this: the rarity of diastrophic dwarves will soon become a significant factor in my life.

■　■　■

JUST AFTER I had recovered from my clubfeet surgery my world changed. For the past several months my parents had been preparing for the arrival of another baby. I remember the hustle and anticipation around the house as a crib was brought in and a room was set up, ready for my new little brother or sister. I also remember my mom being pregnant and feeling the baby kick inside her belly. We were all excited, and I am sure my parents were a bit anxious.

Because the gene that causes dwarfism is recessive, the chances of my parents having another dwarf child were extremely slim. I cannot imagine what went through their minds when, in December of 1977, my brother Toby was born with the same type of dwarfism that I have. This was long before ultrasounds and other tests and procedures that indicated the status of an unborn baby. I can't begin to fathom the shock Toby's birth gave Mom and Dad, but in true Gill fashion they didn't miss a beat. Once again they adapted their plans to make life the best it could be for both of us. I learned a lot from my parents, and the importance of adapting to life's many challenges was a lifelong lesson.

Toby was born with most of the same needs that I had but not the cleft palate, so he was not rushed to Riley as I had been. But because Toby was a breech birth, he was born via an emergency C-section. That meant Mom was laid up longer with Toby than she was with me. Our grandparents, aunts, uncles, and cousins rallied, and life moved on after Toby's arrival.

Even though we are both little people, Toby and I are very different, and that was apparent from the very beginning. My hair is reddish brown and I have bright blue eyes. In fact, Grandpa Wilson used to call me Old Blue Eyes. In contrast, Toby's hair and eyes are dark, like our mom's. My build is stockier than Toby's and even though as adults we are about the same height, Toby's slimmer build allows him to be far more limber than I am.

In personality, I am the outward "go-getter," whereas Toby is more introspective. I usually come up with the ideas, and Toby helps execute them. We complement each other well in that way, although I have to admit I took every advantage of my "big brother" status when we were kids.

While I was rarely jealous of the attention my new little brother was getting, I do remember watching Mom feed Toby in our new La-Z-Boy recliner and being disgusted by the smell of the towel she used to burp him with. However, I loved having a new little brother. Mom did a lot of knitting and her sewing kit was kept on the floor in a basket. One of her favorite stories about me is when I attached a long piece of yarn to Toby's pacifier, then crawled across the room so I could jerk it out of his mouth. That was a fun one! I also used to "comb" Toby's hair with a toy plastic garden rake.

It wasn't long before I realized that Toby could be an asset. By this time Dad had our backyard in pretty good shape. There was a swing set and a sandbox and a lot of room to play. Dad also had a spot for a garden and there was a big cement slab that was our patio.

My mom recalled that, dwarfism aside, I was a "challenging" child to raise. "Fred was busy all the time," she once told a friend. "Being a person who is physically challenged has not slowed him down at all. From the time he was a little boy, he was always working on some project or another."

That was, and is, so true. One of those projects included tying Toby to a table leg while we were in Dr. Blaisedell's office waiting for an appointment. Because of my short arms, to this day I still can't reach my feet to tie my shoes, but when I was four or five I could tie my little brother to a table leg.

Before you start thinking I was an abusive older brother, much of my play with Toby involved getting him to help me build things. Long before the time I turned five, I was designing new toys, and Toby was helpful in holding parts together. Part of my interest in building was adaptive. If we couldn't physically use a toy as it came, I'd add handles or levers or supports to make it work. I'd also invent things that would help Toby and me stand or sit or walk or reach things. Wherever there was a need, I found a way.

This early way of playing has served me well (fantastically well, actually) throughout my life, especially during times when life does not go the way I think it is supposed to. Very early I learned that when something doesn't work for me I need to sit back and think about the situation, and then through trial and error find a way to turn it around to my advantage. I'm not sure I would have figured that out so quickly had it not been for Toby.

■   ■   ■

WHEN TOBY AND I were quite young my dad and his brother-in-law, Rick Trimpe, who was his sister Linda's husband, both worked the late shift at Cummins. Over the years Dad has done just about every job in the plant. My dad, by the way, has been with Cummins for fifty-plus years, longer than anyone except one other employee. That guy has two weeks on my dad. While Dad worked, Mom, Toby, and I spent time at Aunt Linda and Uncle Rick's house, which was about half a mile from ours. They had three daughters, Laura, Jennifer, and Teresa, and they are, respectively, about five, seven, and nine years older than I am. We went to lots of movies with Aunt Linda and "the girls"; they were like sisters to Toby and me.

Dad provided very well for us, even though this meant he often was not home in the evenings or in the morning. That's why when I did get to spend time with him it was all the more special. Much of the time Toby and I spent with him was when he was working.

I remember that the passenger seat of his truck had three little holes in it, tears in the vinyl that proved how well the truck was used. Dad once told me the story of the time he was driving down the road and a big black snake slithered out of the dashboard. After that I was always a little concerned that even though that particular snake was long gone, another would come up through one of the holes in the seat.

Truck driving aside, Dad was also a talented builder. He built our house himself, with help from friends, and did a great job. It's a rock-solid ranch-style home with a crawl space underneath. One day when I was about five, my dad and I went under the house to fix something. I was proud that I could stand up underneath our house and he couldn't. I remember the space where we were working had a light. The other end of the house, however, seemed like a never-ending abyss of darkness that both frightened and intrigued me. All I could see was floor joists fading into the blackness and I was sure the underside of the house led to some unimaginable black hole. While we were under there I didn't get too far away from Dad, but I still talked his ear off.

I don't remember ever expressing those fears to my dad, and that's another thing I have learned along the way: to speak up if I have thoughts or concerns about something. It doesn't do anyone any good to keep things inside. If I had mentioned my fears to Dad he may have been able to show me there was nothing to worry about.

While I was tagging along with Dad whenever I could, Toby was happier being at home with Mom. I can't say it enough: Mom was a saint for all she did for Toby and me. You have to understand that a child typically learns to dress him- or herself at some point early on in life. I couldn't dress myself, use the bathroom privately, or even wipe my own butt until I was twenty-two years old. I couldn't get into bed by myself, flip a light switch, or any of the hundreds of other daily tasks kids do on their own.

I have mixed feelings about this. Mom was understandably watchful of both Toby and me. We needed that, and in her doing for us we both felt safe. In hindsight, however, I wish Mom had allowed and/or pushed us to learn to do things on our own. Looking back, I think we should have learned ways to dress ourselves and use the bathroom long before we actually did. As you will read, I had already graduated from college before I learned a way to do these tasks by myself.

We all have roles in life and Mom was once a daughter. Then she was a student and a teacher and a girlfriend and a wife. When Toby and I came along, while she was still a daughter and a wife, her main role changed to mother and caregiver. For whatever reason, I think she needed that role and was reluctant to relinquish it as we grew older. Without realizing it, she did not want to lose the feeling of being needed that she got from helping us.

Because of our dependence on Mom and others, Toby and I had a lot of structure in our lives that continues with me to this day. Sometimes this causes me a great deal of guilt and anxiety. For example, when we had our shoes put on in the morning, they stayed on until we took our baths at nine P.M. Dinner was always at six o'clock sharp. Today, if I am home for the day and take my shoes off before dinner, if I don't eat until eight, or if I take a shower at one in the afternoon, it feels weird to me—almost as if I should ask permission from someone. In my adult life, I often struggle with, yet relish, the freedom of performing daily tasks in my own time frame.

Eventually, Grandpa Wilson built a little step stool for Toby and me that we put in the bathroom next to the sink and the toilet. We still needed help with going to the bathroom, but the stool helped a lot.

Mom was an only child, and like my dad and his family, she was very close to hers. Most days she managed the challenge of Toby and me with grace and ease, but there were occasions when the challenge got the better of her. When Toby and I had been roughhousing too long she got out the wooden spoon she kept in a kitchen cabinet and spanked us. We usually were so involved in wrestling we didn't hear her ask us to settle down. However, when we heard the cabinet door open we knew right away that one of us was going to get it, so we'd take off.

Toby once hid the spoon—and really well—so Mom, with her teacher instincts, came back with something else to smack us with. I don't want to imply that Mom was abusive; she was quite the opposite. Sometimes a quick swat with a paddle was what Toby or I needed to pay attention.

Our family is Catholic and every Sunday we attended St. Ambrose Catholic Church on South Chestnut Street. St. Ambrose is an old parish with a beautiful sanctuary that was founded in 1860. Mom grew up Baptist, but she converted to Catholicism when she married Dad. We sat in the balcony most Sundays, but on occasion we'd sit toward the back of the church. I have no idea why we sat where we did, other than the fact that St. Ambrose didn't have a "cry room." These locations might have offered Mom and Dad a less visible spot in which to seat two very active young boys who were uninterested in mass.

While we went through the traditional Catholic rituals of baptism, communion, catechism (CCD) classes on Wednesday nights, and confirmation, church for me back then was more of a routine than a God or a worship thing. We were Catholic and that's just what our Catholic family did. I am the last person to tell anyone how to worship or develop his or her relationship with God, but as I grew older I realized that while Catholicism had given me a good foundation, I needed something different. I now consider myself nondenominational and continue to grow in spirituality.

As you might imagine, there was a lot going on in the Gill home during holidays. With all the grandparents and other extended family, we made quite a large crowd. And the food was fabulous. Mom's homemade dressing, what you might call stuffing, was my all-time favorite. I devoured it with barbecue sauce. On Thanksgiving, my cousins' aunt, my uncle Rick's sister Nancy, made a homemade chocolate sheet cake that I *always* looked forward to. It was known throughout our family how much I loved the cake and because of that, Nancy always left me some to snack on later.

Mom and Grandma also made great noodles, and they also baked homemade cinnamon rolls with icing on Christmas morning. And Mom would never stoop to using a store-bought pie or pie crust. That said, if anyone at the table ever complained, Mom was quick with a response to remind us that the food was homemade and that she spent a lot of time cooking it.

Like most kids, Toby and I looked forward to the holidays. Early in December we'd go to a Christmas tree farm to pick out a tree and then we'd go home and decorate it. December was also the time of year when the Sears catalog came out. Some of you might be too young to remember, but for decades families ordered presents not from the Internet, but from the quarterly Sears catalog. Before Christmas, Toby and I inspected the pages dedicated to toys over and over again before choosing our list for Santa. He always came through.

For me, though, one of the best parts of Christmas was getting to spend quality moments with my dad. He worked hard throughout the year to support us, and the holidays were one of the few times we got to spend one-on-one with him. There never was a question as to whether or not he loved us. That was a given, but his work time was precious because it allowed him to give us the nice standard of life we had. Plus, as we got older, Dad typically gave us a really cool gift, a special knife or a rifle, something along those lines. Due to these gifts that often made Mom cringe, I learned to shoot when I was very young and still am a pretty good shot.

■ ■ ■

MY BEST FRIEND at this time of my life was Pat Robinson. He was the same age as I was and his backyard was kitty-corner to ours. We also both attended the Little Red School House preschool, so we got to play together just about every day.

My friendship with Pat taught me several lessons. The first happened in the sandbox at preschool when another kid kicked sand into my eyes. Pat was right there, but he didn't stick up for me. The fact that he didn't defend me stung more than the sand, and I realized that you can't always count on other people, as much as you might like or love them.

The second lesson, however, was far more life-changing. Like my dad, Pat's dad also worked at Cummins. Pat and I had been best buddies all of our young lives so you can imagine my shock when, a few months before I started kindergarten, my parents told me that Pat's dad had been transferred and Pat was moving away.

This was the first major loss in my life. At first I was in disbelief. My secure world had been turned completely upside down. Then my practical side kicked in, and I wanted to know what we had to do to get Pat to stay. Pat and I were supposed to go to kindergarten together, grow up together. There had to be a way. But, of course, there wasn't.

That memory is so very clear, and I now find it interesting that even before I started kindergarten I was trying to negotiate a deal. If we did this or that, then maybe Pat would not move away. My young mind could not register that there was no possibility of Pat staying, but the fact that I tried to make everyone happy, to work out a win-win situation, when I was still in preschool says a lot about how my mind works.

Pat's moving away was a huge blow, but I didn't have too long to dwell on it because kindergarten was right around the corner. Because my birthday was in late July, my parents decided to hold off sending me to kindergarten until I turned six. It turned out to be one of the best decisions they ever made because as I went through school, due to that decision, I was always the first one of my friends to achieve certain milestones. While being first at anything is always an ego booster, it is even more so when you are a person who is different from everyone else around you. These ahead-of-schedule achievements went a long way toward making me a confident adult. But the start of my formal education would not be easy and while I looked forward to it with eager anticipation, the reality was another thing altogether.

3

CREATING FRIENDS FOREVER

I missed my first day of school. Instead of getting on the bus with all the other kids I stayed home, so affected with an allergy to pollen that my eyes were swollen shut. But I didn't have to wait long for the adventure to begin, because I began my formal education the very next day.

I attended morning kindergarten so we had to get up really early. My mom drove me the mile or so down the road to Redding Elementary School. Like a lot of kindergartners, I had anxiety from time to time and at the classroom door I grabbed on to my mom and didn't want to let go, even though I recognized a lot of kids from preschool. My kindergarten teacher, Ms. Crouch, eventually persuaded me to release the death grip I had on my mom's pant leg and I walked into a brand-new world.

My second day of school I rode the bus, and that was the start of a long friendship with Roland "Blondie" Hackman, our bus driver. Although I didn't know it then, Mr. Hackman would be my bus driver through the seventh grade, when I stopped riding the bus to school. He was an older man, a farmer. He and his wife didn't have any children of their own, but he sure knew a lot about kids. Every day when you got on bus number five, you had to shake Mr. Hackman's hand. Talk about teaching respect! Shaking the hand of an adult every school day for eight years does a lot to ingrain manners into a young child.

The bus steps were too high for me to navigate, so Mr. Hackman got out of the bus to pick me up. Every day he'd say, "Are you ready, Freddie?" Then, after shaking hands, he'd deposit me at the top of the steps and I'd walk back to the seat of my choice using each seat cushion as a sort of crutch. I sat all over that bus and got to know everyone who rode it.

All of the kids loved Mr. Hackman; he was by far the coolest bus driver Redding Elementary had. At Christmas he'd give each of us a brown paper bag with an apple, some peanuts, and my favorite, a Snickers bar. The only time I ever saw Mr. Hackman lose his temper was when a kid spit into the metal trash can at the back of the bus. I knew right away that Mr. Hackman was mad because the kid had disrespected Mr. Hackman and the bus enough to behave like that. It only happened the one time, the incident and the anger.

I learned so much from that quiet, humble man and in many ways what I learned from him was far more important than what I learned from my actual teachers. One regret I have (I don't have many) is that after getting my driver's license I often saw Mr. Hackman out and about, and he asked me to come take him for a ride, but I never did before he passed in

2005. I thought about picking him up from time to time but life got in the way and I didn't make it as much of a priority as I should have. I wish now that I had because I know he really would have enjoyed it.

In kindergarten, and also in Mrs. Downing's first-grade class, I was allowed to leave the classroom a few minutes early so I would have time to get to the lunchroom, or art, gym, or music classes. I did not understand why I was allowed this luxury—but I welcomed it. Actually, I always felt as if I was getting away with something, but I didn't dwell on it too much. I was far more interested in the school day coming to an end and seeing Mr. Hackman on my way home.

At lunch I was the one who was always so busy talking that I didn't have time to eat. Not that I didn't like the food that was in my lunchbox; there were just so many people to talk to. I loved it! The prepared meal the school offered on a lunch tray turned my stomach, so in six years of elementary school I never bought a school lunch. Those of you who remember those square pizza slices and awful green beans know what I mean.

Between bites of my peanut butter and jelly sandwich, Doritos, Snickers bar, and lemonade, I got to know the kids sitting around me very well. Sometimes I'd have a peanut butter and Miracle Whip sandwich with some of Grandma Wilson's pickles sliced inside the sandwich. Mom only used Miracle Whip and I was in college before I realized there was another kind of sandwich spread known as mayonnaise.

The school had a point system for lunch to be sure we were getting all the nutrients we needed. I made sure I got all my points even though my lunch didn't quite qualify. I counted the cheese on the Doritos as a dairy product, the jelly on my sandwich as a fruit, and the peanut butter as a meat.

By this time, asking for help came naturally to me, and while I knew I couldn't do some things that other kids did, I hadn't completely put together yet that my body was much different. I just knew I was short and needed help in certain things. My family and I went to occasional Little People of America meetings at the Emkeses' house in Seymour and I saw all shapes and sizes of people there. Outside of that I was living in a world of average-sized people. That's just the way life was and I didn't give it too much thought.

With my kind of dwarfism, while exercise is good for me, too much or the wrong kind can be hard on my joints. But you know what? A lot of people, such as Mr. Myers, our gym teacher, worked hard to keep me involved in the same activities as the rest of my class. My point is that early on in elementary school I was learning that my experience in life was going to be a little different (okay, a lot different) than most people's experience, but that difference wasn't necessarily any better or worse. It was just different.

■   ■   ■

FOR ME, THE start of school marked the beginning of many freedoms as well as many limitations. I am naturally gregarious and thrived on the group atmosphere and the many new activities. But the realities of everyday school life forced me to be creative and to find new coping skills. For example, in first grade, instead of carrying my lunch box I pushed it along the ground in front of me and used it as a tool to help me walk.

By second grade I had settled in to school very well. I found I loved all of the extracurricular classes, especially art with Mrs. Bowman. I was such a hands-on kind of learner that I was not so much interested in history or museums. Reading about the Battle of Gettysburg? Not for me. I'd rather go there. I found math necessary (or so they told me) and science interesting, although as an adult the opposite is true. I now am an avid number cruncher, am very interested in history, and am far less interested in science. But back then I really was as happy and secure as any child could be.

However, something happened about that time that changed the shape of the world for me. This was my first issue with trust and it had to do with my allergies. For a number of years I had allergy shots every Friday afternoon after school. This was understandably a cause for anxiety because the shots hurt.

The routine of the shot was always the same. The nurse would clean off my arm with an alcohol swab and then I'd count down as we had previously agreed to do. Part of the agreement included me not moving and not stopping the countdown. Ten, nine, eight . . . all the way to my saying, "Go." Then she'd give me the shot as we had agreed. On this day, for some reason when I got to three, the nurse, who happened to be new, nailed me. Perhaps she didn't trust me not to move as much as I trusted her to give me the shot at the appropriate time. I don't know, and honestly, I don't really care.

The result was that I lost my trust in her, and in most other people I did not know well. I did not understand why the nurse did not hold up her end of the bargain. I was the one who was getting the painful shot and the countdown helped me prepare for it. Because she jabbed me before the agreed-upon time, it introduced me to the concept that people might not always do what they say they are going to. Everyone learns that lesson along the path of life, but in my perfect world, it may have come a little too early.

The lack of trust also fed into a control issue that I struggle with to this day. That is a losing battle for sure, and it is not healthy for anyone. Having input into certain situations satisfies my need for control. And it's not big things I need to control but the little details. For example, while traveling I feel the need to pick the gas station based on knowing whether or not the chain has decent bathroom facilities that I can use. All of the major truck stops have handicapped-accessible bathrooms, but a mom-and-pop station may not.

My second-grade teacher was Miss Winslow, who happened to be a longtime friend of my mom's. They were both from Franklin, Indiana, and their parents had also been friends for many years. Although I had been able to find alternative ways to do most things at school, I still needed assistance in the bathroom— and would need help for many years to come. (My arms were not long enough to pull my pants down by myself and my fingers weren't long or limber enough to work any buttons, snaps, or zippers on my jeans.) By this time, my daily routine included going number two in the bathroom before leaving for school in the morning. Because of the need to have people who were sometimes near-strangers help me, it was fortunate that I did not have to go during the day.

But I still had good old number one to deal with. One day in class, I knew I had to use the bathroom. We were in a reading session, so I did not tell Miss Winslow as soon as I should have. By the time I told her, she was momentarily preoccupied with something else. I waited a few minutes, but before I could ask her again for help I created a rather large wet spot below me.

This kind of situation happens occasionally in kindergarten to lots of children, but by second grade it is a pretty rare occurrence. I was not ashamed or humiliated, as you might think. I do remember, though, the utter helplessness that I felt. I was also aware that my mom was not pleased when she had to bring me a pair of dry pants. And I was unhappy that Miss Winslow did not take the time to help me when I needed it. It was fortunate that I was about as secure and confident as a kid could be so this event did not have the profound effect it might have had with other kids of that age.

I learned several things that day. One, I needed to prepare not only myself for an action, such as going to the bathroom, I needed to prepare those around me in plenty of time for a successful completion of the job, so to speak. In this case, the accident was not entirely Miss Winslow's fault. I had not given her enough time to prepare, and I assigned myself part of the blame. Enter *the need for control.*

To avoid similar scenarios in the future, I knew I needed a different plan. I could not always rely on my teachers to take time from their classroom. This is where my outgoing nature helped me tremendously. Because I knew so many people, I found it easy to enlist one or two boys who could help me with bathroom duties if my teacher was tied up with other students. That was the beginning of several lifelong friendships.

One was with Travis Trueblood. Travis was in my fourth-grade class and became my first regular bathroom helper. In elementary school, the urinals went all the way down to the floor. This was good because I could use the bathroom without having to stand on anything to reach the urinal. So whenever I had to use the bathroom, Travis would go with me and pull my pants down. I'd pee and then Travis would pull my pants up and we'd return to class. Okay, sometimes we messed around or took detours, but most of the time we returned right away.

■　■　■

WHILE TRAVIS AND a few other boys were my closest friends at school, at home, after school, I'd play with my friends and neighbors David and Angie. The McKains, David's family, lived next door to us, and Angie's family, the Champs, lived on the other side of David's. The four of us grew up as close as siblings, and to this day Angie works for my company. Angie is Toby's age and David is younger than I am but older than Toby.

I remember that David came over after school just about every day. We built forts and it was always David and Toby against me. With my competitive nature I don't have to tell you who won most of the battles. In good weather we ran amok in the backyard, but if it was cold or wet outside we'd steal cushions from the couch and beg Mom for sheets and other covers to build our forts.

During the summer we'd all spend the day in one of our backyards building something and then tearing it apart, or burning leftover plants or something in my dad's garden. I loved to burn things. We played cars and trucks, war, and a game we invented called detective. Angie, too. We modified the backyard to our needs, sometimes to the despair of our parents.

In between playing with friends such as David and Angie, Toby and I rode the plastic tricycles that we received for Christmas one year, what we called our "hot rods." We turned them into our way of being mobile and raced around the neighborhood. We also used them to get around stores, when we went out to eat, and on vacation.

Toby and I also wrestled a lot. As we got older we were always about the same size, so we could not unintentionally inflict the kind of damage on each other that average-sized boys might. Except for one time when Toby was about four.

Around this time Toby had an issue with his neck that took six weeks to diagnose. After weeks of testing, doctors at Riley Children's Hospital finally determined that they needed to take a bone graft out of his leg and put it into his neck. This happened when I was eight. Toby and Mom were at Riley for months, during which I spent all my time at Aunt Linda's. Dad occasionally picked me up from school in the dump truck to go to a restaurant called Betty's Townhouse for lunch, which I hated, but I liked being with Dad. He and I also went to visit Mom and Toby every weekend, oftentimes picking up Grandma and Grandpa Wilson in Franklin on the way. When Toby came home his head and neck were in full traction and supported by a metal "halo" that had bolts that went into Toby's head. This was all supported by a full-body cast.

One day around the holidays we were horsing around on our hot rods and I pushed Toby over. The result was that the fall caused one of the bolts to move farther into Toby's temple and there was fluid oozing around the bolt. It was a traumatic thing for all of us except Toby. He couldn't understand what the fuss was about.

Right away Mom called Dad at work in Columbus. Then Dad called the state police and told them what was going on. Back then, you didn't think to call an ambulance, you just went. The end result was that Mom, Dad, and Toby had a police escort all the way to Indianapolis as they rushed Toby back to Riley. Luckily it was about time for the rods to be removed anyway and the doctors took them off.

I can't tell you the guilt and remorse I felt. Man, did I feel bad. I had intentionally pushed Toby off the tricycle, but I had not intended for him to get hurt. That incident made me realize the importance of thinking things through.

So often our actions have unintended results. Now I try to think of every possible outcome to a scenario before I act. I can't always predict the results, but I can say that instances of my hurting someone are rare. But it took more than just Toby for me to get there. It also took the devastating loss of a friendship and help of a teacher.

SMASHING THROUGH THE WALLS OF PERCEPTION

Around third grade I began riding around school on a wheeled device one of the teachers had ordered for me from a special catalog. The device was like a long, wide skateboard with handles at one end. I'm sure the intention of the teacher was for me to push it by myself, but the situation quickly turned into one where numerous kids volunteered to push me while I rode. Again, I felt I was getting away with something that was privileged, but more recently I turned that thought sideways. Now I realize the device was a precursor to the motorized scooter I use today, making me as mobile as the people around me.

In the meantime, I was enamored with an Apple IIc computer that belonged to Redding Elementary. It was the only computer the school had and I nagged and nagged my teacher to put our classroom on the waiting list so we could use it. I was quite taken with the new experience that computer provided, so you can imagine my excitement when our family got one for Christmas. We had that computer a long time and I used it just about every day, even though it didn't do much other than run basic games and word processing programs.

This must seem absurd now, but you have to remember that the early 1980s was a time when few people had a computer at home. Our school had one book in the library pertaining to computers and I checked it out over and over, to the point that our librarian, Mrs. McIntosh, asked me if I was going to turn the book in when the school year was over.

My interest in computers was excessive but at the time, I felt it was underappreciated by the adults around me. And that lack of understanding from others just fueled the fire of my interest. For a time, I wanted to eat, live, and breathe computers. It was my first experience with obsessive behavior, although no one close to me, including myself, realized it. Unfortunately, it was a foreshadowing of many obsessions, including drinking, gambling, and women. They would all be expensive lessons, but those days were yet to come.

■　■　■

AS I MATURED, my middle elementary school years were filled with normal childhood activities such as Boy Scouts and memorable summer breaks.

Toby, my friends, and I often played baseball with a tennis ball. I also played T-ball and one of my coaches, Dan Meek, who was also the assistant director at the Boys Club, made a special tee and bat for me. Steve Stanfield, who was the director at the Boys Club, was also very supportive. I remember one particular day when my dad drove up in his dump truck to watch part of one of my games. It was huge for him to take part of his workday to come watch me play, but it was an even bigger deal for me.

Other than hunting, Dad was not a sports kind of guy, so Dan was the one who taught me to hit. He was a pretty good hitting coach because I got on base a few times. Man, that felt good! That small success kept me pumped up for the rest of the day. I realize now that the coaches and other players had previously discussed "letting" me get on base even though I ran slowly. But, that would not have happened if I had not been able to hit the ball in the first place. Our team was the Cubs and one year we won the league championship. I loved being part of the team.

As the years passed, the difference in size between the other kids and me was becoming more extensive, so I became more adept at being equipment manager, scorekeeper, and head motivator at school. I still participated in, and often organized and coached, our neighborhood games that we played in the then-vacant lot on the other side of the subdivision.

During this time I was also heavily involved in Scouting. So much so that I eventually became an Eagle Scout, the highest ranking a Boy Scout can achieve. Scouts offered me the structure I was used to, along with friendship, interaction, learning, and adventure—all things I love to this day.

I loved working on most of the merit badges, especially the kind where you built stuff. I have always loved a good project. Marksmanship, however, was one of my favorite merit badges.

Some of the Scouting events and requirements were difficult for me, though. Think hiking or rock climbing. There was no way. Camping presented special challenges as someone else had to carry my gear, and if the campground was not someplace I could be dropped off or reach with my scooter, it was about impossible for me to participate. The whole culture of Scouts is to help other people and that worked for me quite well, as my fellow Scouts were willing to lend a hand whenever they could.

Not getting a merit badge wasn't always due to my physical limitations, though. I remember working on my aviation merit badge. We had to go to a special class several Saturday mornings in a row that was taught by a local pilot. I did not take the class seriously and did not pass the test. Consequently, I did not get that merit badge. Mom was not happy, but I learned something from that experience. You have to pay attention and focus in order to achieve a goal.

You might think I felt sad that I did not actively participate in the games as a player or in some Scout activities. But I didn't. My thought process was that one of these days I was going to do something that would dwarf all of those missed activities. My being on the sidelines of most things that involved athleticism just . . . was.

While I participated in organized activities such as sports and Scouting, a group of friends and I also often spent the night at each other's houses, which I eagerly anticipated. Or at least I did until one particular sleepover.

On this particular day, my family and I had just gotten home from a trip when my good friend Jason McDaniel called to see if I wanted to spend the night. I loved spending the night at my friends' houses and having them sleep over at mine. This was going to be so much fun.

I really wanted to go, but Mom initially said no. Then I whined and whined until Mom reluctantly changed her mind. I thought at the time that she was being mean and I couldn't understand why she didn't want me to go, when in reality she just wanted to spend time with me, and with our family, at home.

Just so you know, when people came over to my house for a sleepover, Mom had our sleeping bags out and ready to go. Snacks were prepared and in place. Activities were planned. In short, there was structure. A lot of it. And that's what I was used to.

Jason lived in an adjoining neighborhood to ours and was one of five kids, and wow, there was no structure whatsoever. I mean, it was a free-for-all over there. Jason was the oldest, then he had a younger brother and sister, and brothers who were twin toddlers. So instead of a nice and neat row of sleeping bags and plenty of snacks, kids were running all over the place. In hindsight, Jason's house was probably relatively organized and not the mob scene I remember. It's just that the extreme structure in my home and the rowdy group in his were polar opposites.

The big problem was that I became sick with guilt that I had talked Mom into letting me do something she didn't want me to. My guilt grew so big that, after just an hour or so, I became sick to my stomach and asked Jason's dad to take me home.

To my mom's surprise I showed up on our doorstep not too long after she dropped me off at Jason's and she never knew why, other than I told her I was sick. We were not the kind of family who talked about feelings a lot, or about many of the important things in life, so I was uncomfortable with the thought of confessing my guilty feelings to her. I was also disappointed in myself that I felt that way.

Jason also never knew why I didn't stay that night. I'm sure he thought he did something wrong.

It was a long time before I spent the night at someone else's house again. In fact, I don't remember that I ever did. Since then I have come full circle. I can eat, sleep, or use the bathroom anywhere, anyplace, anytime without the terrorizing feeling of helplessness and guilt that I felt that evening at Jason's.

But that evening was not the end of my guilt. There was an episode in fifth or sixth grade when I was at recess. Because of my allergies, I usually carried a little box of Kleenex with me. On this day, however, I didn't have any. Mom was called and she brought a new box to school. While she was there I saw her down the hall from my room but I did not say hi to her. That brought on another huge bout of guilt and in the middle of my after-school duties as timekeeper for the basketball team I told the coach I had to go home. I knew Mom had seen me and I was so worried that she was disappointed in me because I did not say hi to her. My guilt was so huge that I had to be sure Mom was not upset with me.

I am not sure where all my guilt came from. Was it a Catholic thing? Or was it just me? I didn't have too long to dwell on it, though, because something else was coming into play in my life. Structure.

As I've mentioned, our household—and my life—was very structured. CCD for our Catholic church was always on Wednesday nights. The reason we attended this class was that we did not go to Catholic grade school, since it was on two levels and we could not get up and down the steps. There were no nuns at our church, so a mother of a kid in the class usually taught it. I have to say I have learned more about spirituality, God, and the Bible in the last eighteen months than I ever did in CCD class.

Every Thursday I went to Cub Scouts. Mothers also led these meetings—den mothers. The one time during the year my dad got involved with Cub Scouts was during the Pinewood Derby race. This is a huge national event divided into regions where each Scout is given a kit that includes wheels and a block of wood. Scouts then design and paint a race car from that piece of wood. The race consists of releasing multiple cars to roll down a uniform track and is a single elimination event. This means if you lost once, you and your car were out. After several rounds, the last car standing is determined the winner.

I spent what seemed like a million hours sanding my wedge of a car. Other kids designed their cars to look cool, like police cars, real race cars, or antique cars. I didn't care what my car looked like. I just wanted it to be fast. Really fast. And it was. My car not only won for my local area, it won the state championship. The races were extremely competitive so it was a really big deal. Dad helped me some with it and I remember how special I felt that he took time out of his busy schedule to do this. It was one of the few times we could celebrate a mutual achievement together.

Getting back to structure. As you can see, back then my daily and weekly consistency was so ingrained that I felt lost without it. The structure of my early years stays with me to this day, and I'm not altogether sure it is a good thing.

The one time my regulated life relaxed a little was in the summer. Toby, my friends, and I had the run of our neighborhood and we made full use of that liberty. From a very young age I had a go-kart that Dad modified for us, and Toby and I rode miles in circles around our neighborhood. We played war and hung out in one house or another watching TV or playing games.

One summer Mom signed me up for swimming lessons at the Seymour city pool. I was excited about this opportunity because no one had a pool. Just being in a swimming pool was cool and the lessons guaranteed I'd be there twice a week. If I could learn to swim, then when I was in the water I could be just as mobile as anyone else. The important word here was "if."

I did not do well with my first swim instructor, who was a summer lifeguard and in college. For some reason I could not grasp the necessary concepts or make my body relax enough to float. This failure just served to make me more uptight and I began to dread the thought of swimming. After a while I actually became terrified, which is never a good thing when you are in the water. Thank goodness Dan Meek once again stepped in and turned the situation around.

Dan began giving me private lessons in a kiddie swimming pool where I felt safe and secure because I could stand up. He patiently did that after my other lesson on his own time. Dan showed me the strokes and taught me to relax enough that I could trust myself in just one foot of water. Every day the water in that little pool got a little deeper and before I knew it I was swimming like a fish in the big pool with the rest of the kids. In fact, one of my goals in learning to swim had been to jump off the diving board. Was I ever proud the first time I did that! And you know what? It was every bit as fun as I thought it would be.

I am so indebted to Dan. He didn't have to take the time to help me, but he did. He believed in me, believed I could learn to swim when even I was starting to wonder whether I could or not. Everyone needs a champion and that summer Dan Meek was mine. Thanks to him I still enjoy swimming and going to the Y regularly to use their pool. I can also handle myself pretty well in a hot hub—even one occasionally filled with ladies.

■ ■ ■

BY THE TIME fourth grade rolled around I was quite the confident kid. But in many ways I was like a bull in a china shop. I was all energy and no finesse, and my main goal in life was to have fun. My self-esteem was through the roof and I felt comfortable in school and in my routines. But I wanted more out of life. Little did I know that in a roundabout way, I was going to get just that.

That year Lanny McCune was my teacher. He was my first male teacher and in fact, before I saw him in my fourth-grade homeroom class, I'm not sure I ever considered the idea that a guy could be my everyday teacher. It turned out that having Mr. McCune as my teacher was meant to be. He not only pushed me to become more independent, he gave me the belief that I could do more on my own.

I mentioned earlier that Travis Trueblood was a friend who helped me use the bathroom at school. In the middle of fourth grade, Travis and I had a petty squabble over something that neither one of us remembers and we went our separate ways. After the argument, I realized that this was much more than just the breakup of a friendship. Travis was key in my independence. Before Travis began to help me, teachers assisted me in the bathroom. I did not want to go back to that, but without Travis, what would I do?

This was one of the first times I remember looking inward and contemplating my unique personality. I tried to figure out what had happened between Travis and me and I realized that while I was filled with gratitude for my friends and my family, maybe I also felt a little too entitled to being helped. This is an advanced concept for a fourth grader, to be sure, but maybe not for a person with a physical difference such as mine. Out of necessity, I have to navigate the world somewhat differently, and when you tie a friendship in to a basic human function such as using the bathroom, life becomes infinitely more complicated no matter how old you are.

Jason McDaniel began helping me in the bathroom and this simple act of kindness made me appreciate both Jason and Travis all the more. It also opened the door to the fact that I could accept help from many more people than I ever thought possible. Plus, my feelings of entitlement slowly changed to feelings of gratitude.

The end result was that through this new subconscious idea of accepting help, I could play at the homes of more friends. I could go to the movies more, and with kids I didn't know as well. The situation that began with a childhood quarrel and the potential loss of a friendship actually opened many doors for me.

I say potential loss of a friendship, because when it came

to Travis, Mr. McCune stepped in and rectified the situation. It took a little time, but through the work of a caring teacher, Travis and I eventually became better friends than we had ever been.

Jason and I had our differences too, especially when it came to my first love, Betsy Bridges. Betsy was a cute blue-eyed blonde who lived just outside of our little neighborhood, but with easy access to our subdivision if we cut through a few neighbors' yards. I first met her in preschool and we were friends, but by the fourth grade we were at the flirting/fighting stage.

One time when I was at Jason's house I asked him if he liked girls and he said yes. That's when I confessed that I "liked" Betsy, not knowing that Jason liked her, too. I had some sincere fourth-grade angst when I realized we both liked the same girl. It worked out though, because Betsy chose to remain friends with both of us. It was an early inkling of my future, or lack thereof, with women.

■ ■ ■

WHILE SCHOOL WAS okay, and I liked seeing Betsy, my favorite time of the week was the weekend. On Friday nights I'd get out the TV section of the paper, get a lined index card, and map out my cartoon schedule for the next morning. First up was *Kids Incorporated* at seven thirty, which was followed by *The Smurfs* and several other popular cartoons.

Back then we had a cable box on the floor next to the TV. To change the channel, you turned a dial on the box. I loved living in Seymour, Indiana, for a lot of reasons, but one big perk was that we got both the Indianapolis, Indiana, and the Louisville, Kentucky, stations. And, because we didn't follow daylight savings time as many other areas of the country did, we got to watch each show twice, one an hour later than the other. How cool was that?

On a funny side note, I didn't realize until I was in college that not everyone had two versions of ABC, NBC, and CBS. We usually watched the Indianapolis stations, but if something really good was on, we'd watch it again on the Louisville channel. This, of course, was before DVRs, Internet television, or even taping shows on a VCR to watch later.

Part of the Saturday-morning cartoon ritual was eating a Hostess Ding Dong. These were chocolate-coated cream-filled goodies that were wrapped in aluminum foil. I had a ritual to unwrapping the foil that was so much cooler than opening the plastic-wrapped Ding Dong of today. It's just not the same, and that includes the taste. A while ago I wrapped a Ding Dong in aluminum foil and stuck it in my freezer for about a month. When I unwrapped and ate it, it closely resembled the treat of my youth. If I could get my Ding Dongs wrapped in aluminum like they used to be, I'd accept any supposed health risk the aluminum might cause.

In addition to choosing the snacks, being almost four years older than Toby, I picked all of the shows we watched. In addition to cartoons, we watched *The A-Team, The Andy Griffith Show, Diff'rent Strokes*, and *The Facts of Life*. We also watched *The Brady Bunch* every day after school and *The Dukes of Hazzard* on Friday nights.

I especially liked the character Jo on *The Facts of Life* and

Gary Coleman on *Diff'rent Strokes,* and I was crazy about Bo and Luke Duke on *The Dukes of Hazzard.* If someone had told my ten-year-old self that someday I would get to kiss the actress who played Daisy Duke, kiss Marcia Brady, meet the entire cast of *The Dukes of Hazzard,* and call the actors who played Rosco P. Coltrane on *Dukes* and Goober on *Andy Griffith* friends, it would have blown me away. In fact, it still blows me away. George Lindsey (Goober) and I appeared on Larry the Cable Guy's television show a few years back and I was extremely stunned and honored when "Goober" asked if he could take a picture with me.

Sitting in our living room in Seymour during the 1980s, I never in a million years would have guessed any of that would have happened. And it wouldn't for a while yet. I had a major surgery coming up and a lifetime of experiences to get through first. I had no idea what I was in for.

5

FAMILY, SURGERY, AND PRAYER

The summer before seventh grade I got an electric three-wheeled scooter to help with my mobility. As I've mentioned, due to my size and proportionately short arms and legs it is difficult for me to walk long distances or to get anywhere quickly on my own. Plus, too much exercise is hard on my joints.

Mom had been shopping an hour away at a mall in Indianapolis when she saw a kiosk for Electric Mobility, which sold Rascal scooters. Until then, Mom didn't know an electric scooter with a seat that people used to gain mobility even existed. After inquiring about it, a salesman brought one to our house and I remember thinking if Mom and Dad didn't buy this electric wonder, I would just die. The mobility it would give me was going to be incredible. I was hooked. Mom and Dad must have been too, because when the salesman left the scooter stayed with us.

We had no way to easily transport the scooter, so during the school year my new wheels lived in the office at school. During vacations we'd bring it home and Toby and I shared it, or we'd ride together on it. I can't tell you the difference this scooter made in my life. All of a sudden I could keep up with my classmates on my own. This was a big deal because for seventh grade I started attending Seymour Middle School. In middle school each subject was in a different classroom so I had to travel around the school a lot.

In addition, former sixth graders from five different elementary schools were now crowding the hallway. With my scooter, I was on the same level as everyone else. I could carry my own books with me in a basket in the front. I had control over where I went and when, because I didn't have to wait for other people to come push me on the wheeled device I'd used before. If I wanted, for example, to stop to chat with someone, I could. I didn't have to worry that whoever was pushing me might need to stop to use the restroom or not have time to drop me off and then go to a different classroom. What a life-changer!

The scooter was also a life-changer for Mom and Dad. With two kids facing the challenges of diastrophic dwarfism, you can imagine that they were often spread thin—with much of that being physically. But living in small-town America means everyone knows everyone else. Without our extended family, neighbors, friends, and of course the scooter, I don't know how my parents would have gotten through.

My mom's cousin Charlotte was a big help emotionally. Charlotte's mom had died when Charlotte was still a young adult. Because my mom was an only child, she and Mom became as close as sisters. Their relationship showed me that anyone can become your immediate family, as long as they earn that honor. Charlotte did, and to this day still does.

Even though they lived about forty miles away, Grandma and Grandpa Wilson were also around a lot. Grandpa Wilson was the kind of man who paid cash for quality and took care of his things. Even though I watched and admired the way he lived his life with quiet dignity, unfortunately, I haven't always followed his example. That is to my detriment and I now know what an important example he set for me.

Grandma and Grandpa Gill lived in town. Grandpa Gill was the kind of guy who'd come over, ask for your car keys with no explanation, and return your car washed and with a full tank of gas. His doing kind things for people for no other reason than he cared about them and wanted to make them happy is something that I appreciated, but it has taken maturity for me to learn and practice this.

And then, of course, there was Aunt Linda. Toby and I were in and out of her home almost as much as we were ours. She and my cousins, the girls, often stepped in when life got to be a little too crazy.

■ ■ ■

MY FIRST TWELVE years were basically spent going from surgery to surgery, from one annual doctor's appointment to the next. Once a year, Mom, Toby, and I went to Riley Children's Hospital, where we sat through a number of doctor's appointments and X-rays. We also went every two years or so to have our Boston Braces refitted.

A Boston Brace is a heavy full-torso brace that is molded to your body from chin to hip. It limits movement of the spine and hopefully slows the curvature associated with scoliosis. Until I was twelve, I slept in my brace every single night that I couldn't talk my way out of it. I hated that brace. I remember intentionally scratching my chest in the shower hard enough to make red marks. That irritated my skin so badly that I couldn't wear the brace.

It was important that my brace be a good fit so my internal organs did not become compromised. So the three of us, along with Grandma Wilson (and sometimes Grandma Gill), sat in a tiny, sterile room while the fittings were done. I know Toby and I drove the adults nuts. Neither of us was any good at waiting patiently or quietly.

After the fittings and all the other appointments, we'd go to Toys "R" Us and pick out something really cool, like a Nintendo, Atari, or Sega game. We did not have anything close to a Toys "R" Us in Seymour, so it was a huge deal for us to get to go to a store like that.

While we loved the store and the toys we got there, the reality of why Toby and I were there in the first place inadvertently taught me that I had to have something bad happen to me before I could get something good. As an adult, I have had to restructure my thought process and, I have to say, it's been hard. I've realized that I am still learning how to receive. This has affected my life in many ways, including personal and business relationships, and also my more-than-PG-rated adult behavior.

We knew surgery to correct my spine curvature was in the future, but until the summer before I was in seventh grade, every year during my annual appointment we'd be told to wait until next year, and then "we'd see." One reason for the wait was because the surgery fused the spine and that stopped growth, so we needed to gain as much height as we could before the operation. There is a fine line between doing the surgery too soon and waiting too long. If Toby and I waited too long, then we could have lifelong neurological troubles, and troubles with our internal organs. This is because the extreme curvature of the spine could push organs out of place.

The days of those appointments were filled with a lot of anxiety. First, we'd get up very early. Mom would get Toby and me ready, and then she'd put on her perfume, Chanel No. 5. I dreaded smelling the perfume, because I knew in just moments we'd be on our way. Mom only wore that perfume if she was going to an important place, such as our doctor's office.

I have such a vivid memory of that time period. We'd drive from Seymour to Franklin, pick up Grandma Wilson, and then make the additional twenty-minute drive to Indianapolis. Those twenty minutes always seemed like twenty hours, and for me they were filled with dread. Would this be the day we were given the go-ahead for the surgery?

At the hospital, we'd park and then unload whatever mode of transportation Toby and I used for mobility. At first it was strollers pushed by Grandma and Mom. Later it was our self-propelled hot rods and then our scooters. After parking we checked into the doctor's office, which was a cold, sterile-smelling room with more kids than toys. Then we'd head to X-ray.

Back then the X-ray process took several hours. Toby and I about went wacko from boredom. Grandma Wilson tried to keep us occupied with endless card games of crazy eights. Later she taught us how to play solitaire.

Eventually an orderly would come for one of us, and we'd head to a bigger, colder room. When it was my turn, I was stripped to my underwear and asked to bend into a number of awkward and sometimes painful positions for what seemed like minutes on end so they could get all kinds of different views of my spine. During each X-ray I could see the bright crosshatches projected on my body, and later it reminded me of *The Incredible Hulk* when David Banner did the X-rays on himself. For a number of years I had no protection, such as a lead apron, over my private parts. The people doing the testing wore lead aprons, but I was given no protection whatsoever. As an adult it makes me wonder if being exposed to that much radiation will have an effect on me over time or not.

After the X-rays we went back to the waiting area . . . and waited. Sometimes Toby or I needed to do a specific pose again. During the wait I about made myself sick worrying that this was the day I'd be told it was time for the surgery.

When we finally got the okay on the X-rays we'd grab lunch in the canteen. Today you'd call it the food court. Then we'd go back to the orthopedic surgeon's office. When we were told this was not the year for the surgery we all breathed a sigh of relief. Then, as after the Boston Brace fittings, we'd go to Toys "R" Us and then have dinner at Grandma and Grandpa Wilson's house.

Grandpa Wilson had also taught us how to shoot BB guns and we sometimes practiced shooting at tin cans in his backyard. It was a great way to de-stress at the end of a long day and to this day I love to shoot.

The summer I turned thirteen, we got the dreaded answer—it was time. The surgery was scheduled for just after the first of the year, and it turned out that I was to have two surgeries. The first was to remove one of my left ribs. This was to make my body pliable enough so I could have the scoliosis surgery, which fused my spine with titanium rods.

My surgeon was a pediatric orthopedist, Dr. Paul DeRosa. He was a large, intimidating man with a big, thick mustache. Everyone at the time and since then has said he was the best. I know now that there are very few coincidences, that everything is part of God's plan, but I have always felt so fortunate to have such a skilled surgeon work on me. Recently, while working out, I had a neck injury and the orthopedic doctor was very impressed with how well my spinal fusion had been done.

During the surgeries I stayed at Riley for several weeks with my mom by my side. Toby stayed with Aunt Linda and he and Dad came to visit us on the weekends. Thanks to a morphine pump that allowed me a new dose every ten minutes, a lot of that time is a blur for me. I had no idea what morphine was, but I remember closing my eyes and picturing myself flying through the walls of our house. I still think that was pretty cool.

When I finally went home I was in a body cast from my armpits to my hips. There was a hole in the belly area and it wasn't too long before it became quite stained and underneath the cast became smelly. There was no option of a shower, so Mom washed me as best she could. Instead of having independence and mobility with my scooter, I was now pushed around in a wheelchair. As you might imagine, I missed a lot of school. Mom had been a teacher before I was born, so we got a lot of work done at home.

I also started drawing a lot of pictures while I was recuperating. But while my intentions were good, I'd start a picture and then lose the energy and interest to finish it. This was a side effect of my medications and my recuperation, but I think now that might be why I am often a starter and not a finisher. To this day I start lots of things that I never finish. Old habits definitely die hard.

After a month or so of wearing the cast, Mom noticed a strange smell, so she and Dad took me to Riley to get it checked out. There, they cut a large, square hole in the cast over my incision for a closer look. With no visible signs of infection their only conclusion was I had probably been wetting the bed and that was what caused the smell. So they patched the cast back up and sent us home.

The diagnosis may have satisfied my medical team, but Mom was skeptical. She knew whether I had wet the bed or not and believed I hadn't. Finally it was time for the cast to come off. When it was cut away I had a huge row of blisters up and down my incision. I remember lying on my side and it felt like Dr. DeRosa was rolling up layers of skin off my back when in reality he was bursting all of the blisters. He showed Mom how to treat me with peroxide and gauze, and we went home.

By this time, Dad had been elected as one of our county commissioners and because of this he was on our local hospital's board of directors. Just after the cast came off Dad was scheduled to attend the annual hospital board retreat in Florida on Sanibel Island and board member families were allowed to go as well. There was some debate as to whether or not I should go—I had strict instructions not to get in the water—but we would be in the company of a few doctors so Mom and Dad felt that was a good safety net.

Even though the cast was off, due to the removal of the blisters my back was still excruciatingly sore and raw. One morning while we were still at the retreat, Mom took the gauze off my incision and was surprised and terribly shocked to find that my skin had deteriorated to the point that she could see through to one of the stabilizing rods they had installed during my surgery. Dad called in one of the doctors who was at the retreat, and after a quick look, he said he thought I'd be okay. Mom also called Dr. DeRosa and he confirmed that it was okay to stay, so Mom continued her use of peroxide and gauze until we returned home a week later.

Mom knew something was terribly wrong, but she stayed strong and didn't give me a reason to worry. As soon as we got home, she and Dad took me to Riley, where they found I had a severe staph infection. If you aren't aware, staph is a potentially deadly bacteria, and I had to have immediate surgery to rid my body of the infection.

I remember being in the operating room asking the doctor questions about staph and what they were about to do. You might think I was nervous, even terrified, but this time I wasn't. I had been up close and personal with my back issues since the surgery and I was so worn down by this point I just wanted it to be over. I was very peaceful as I counted backward waiting for the anesthesia to take effect.

When I woke up after the surgery I had a large piece of Saran Wrap clinging to my back as well as stitches the size of football lacings. I later learned it took a Waterpik-like device and eight gallons of water to clean all the staph out of my back. The first few days I was still very weak, but soon my renewed energy began wearing Mom out once again. She pushed me up and down the hall to the playroom countless times and I had a great time meeting and talking with all the kids. I hadn't felt that good in a long time.

As I healed, I had so much anxiety about the doctors pulling the Saran Wrap off that several days before it was time I started helping the process by peeling the corner of the thick, sticky membrane. When Dr. DeRosa slowly peeled the wrap back, it was excruciating. But as soon as it was over, the pain subsided.

I had more anxiety a few weeks later when it was time for the long line of stitches to come out. Quite frankly, I was scared to death. But that worrying turned out to be wasted energy; I didn't feel a thing. I then began seeing a pediatric infectious disease doctor who put me on two thousand milligrams of the powerful antibiotic Keflex every six hours around the clock for two years. Mom knew the staph infection could have killed me and was diligent about waking me up at four A.M. every day so I would not be late on my dose.

While I have not had any flare-ups with staph since, I was told the bacteria could lie dormant for more than thirty years. I guess time will tell.

■ ■ ■

WHILE THE PHYSICAL ordeal of my surgery was over, the social implications were just beginning. Of all the times to have the surgery done, the second half of my seventh-grade year was not the best. This is the stage in life when kids are maturing socially and beginning to take notice of the opposite sex. I missed out on a lot of that and sometimes I still feel as if I am trying to catch up.

The first half of the year, a lot of us went to movies in groups. Mom would drop Travis and/or Jason and me off at the Jackson Park Cinema, we'd go to the movie, and then we'd get some pizza next door at Noble Roman's. By the second semester, most of my friends had paired off into boy/girl partners. Of course, I missed most of that as I was home during my recovery.

When I finally got back to school I felt like a fifth wheel in social situations. To make matters worse, it was beginning to dawn on me in new ways that my body was quite different from the bodies of most of my friends. Top that with the usual angst and hormone overload of a boy that age and I have to say, I was confused. My go-getter attitude and my gregarious personality are probably the only things that got me through that time in my life.

I still was headstrong. I was still quite naïve. But during this time my mentality of equality took a backseat to insecure physical neediness—more than I had ever experienced before. To say I was taken aback by these developments is an understatement. I was in many ways my own worst enemy. I remember going out behind the movie theater after the movie to sit on the sidelines and watch as my friends and the girls played spin the bottle. I also remember being mad at the lack of inclusiveness and having thoughts that one day I would buy and sell them all, that someday they were going to wish they were me. That was my way of coping with what I now know is insecurity.

This also was a time when my guy friends began to do things that excluded me. Until now, Travis, Jason, and I had been like the Three Musketeers, and I remember how bad I felt when the two of them went to Kings Island theme park for a birthday celebration without me. Now, I realize I was not invited because I could not ride all the rides. In fact, it would have been dangerous for me to do so. But I did not know that then. Then, all I felt was left out.

I didn't get depressed. That would come later—in fact, twice. But I did feel that I was living in a world that sometimes excluded me and did not give me the opportunities I so wished I had, mainly with girls. It was an emotional time that I look back on as one of the most difficult in my life. If I knew then what I know now I would have realized that seventh grade is far from easy for most adolescents. I was being much harder on myself than I should have been, which has been a common theme through my life.

■ ■ ■

TODAY I HAVE enough perspective to look at my surgeries and the aftermath thereof with amazement. While it seemed at the time as if it was one blow after the other, I can see now that I was able to meet each challenge one at a time. This is a strategy that I have used quite often since then. Specifically, these early life challenges taught me how to deal with what I call an "Ostrichitis mentality." Ostrichitis is a term I coined that refers to the act of putting one's head in the sand and hiding from a problem, rather than dealing with it head-on. Ostriches have a powerful forward kick that, if they choose, can be used to defend themselves or attack another animal. What this means is that problems and negative situations do not go away without some active input from you. I had to pull my head out of the sand and start kicking.

Although I realized what most of the problems were, I did not have all the answers. I knew there were things in my life that I could not change, specifically my body. I also knew I could affect how people reacted to my body and to me. Now I just had to figure out how to do that.

6

REJECTION FUELS AN ENTREPRENEURIAL SPIRIT

I had an entrepreneurial spirit from a very young age and while I didn't realize it at the time, my interest in the creative side of business was a key component in my learning how to adapt to life's many unique scenarios, including interaction with the opposite sex.

About this time I began organizing projects that had the potential to make some money. A few years back I had learned an important lesson about business and life when Toby and I began collecting empty aluminum cans that I sold back to an aluminum recycling company. I quickly realized that it took a lot of empty cans to make up a pound of aluminum.

One day I had the "brilliant" idea of adding sand to the cans to make them weigh more. In my eleven-year-old mind, the more weight we had to sell, the more money we'd make. I didn't think beyond that, but fortunately Grandpa Wilson did. I'll never forget the day I bragged to him that I had found a way to make more money. Right away he said, "That's not the way you should operate. That's cheating. For right's and wrong's sake that's not the right thing to do, and besides, they know how much a barrel of cans should weigh."

I had not considered the situation from that angle before and it was a giant lesson for me in integrity. So big, in fact, that I will never forget it.

I was very excited about making money because I wanted "stuff." While I had a golden tongue for talking my parents into seeing my point of view when I wanted something, they didn't always have enough money for everything I wanted. Having my own money meant financial independence and more free-dom to pick and choose for big-ticket items. After the talk with Grandpa Wilson, however, I knew I'd have to find an additional way to increase my income. The financial return on can col-lecting was too low to suit my purposes. Even then I was a big thinker.

The next venture I started was with my friend Jason, when we decided to open up a zoo. No one in Seymour ever had a zoo before, I thought. We were sure to make a killing. Jason and I both had pet rabbits, and between us and a few other neighbor-hood friends, we rounded up several dogs, cats, gerbils, ham-sters, guinea pigs, and I think there was even a turtle. The zoo was in Jason's backyard and ended up being more of a petting zoo. As with the can collecting, this turned out to be another great learning experience, but with no real income potential.

Both Jason and I were disappointed that only a few people came. We couldn't figure it out. We spent a lot of time setting the zoo up but only a few experienced it. As we only charged a nickel admission, splitting the proceeds from our meager sales gave us each about fifteen cents. Big bummer. But because of the zoo I learned the importance of marketing and advertising. If you have a great product, you have to find a way to let people know about it. I didn't know how to make that happen yet, but I now realized those things were an important part of any business plan.

I next decided to have a carnival at my house. The carnival was a fun way for us to get rid of smaller toys and games. To do that we set up games such as darts and a ring-toss, and gave away toys as prizes. We once again charged a nickel but found we had a much bigger turnout because the kids who came were getting something tangible. From the carnival I learned that it is hard to quantify the value of petting a rabbit, but when you are able to take home a cool new toy, well, that's perceived as being worth something. I stored that important bit of knowledge for future reference.

The carnival turned out to be a big deal and there were tons of kids running around our backyard. I am sure Mom watched the entire plan develop with horror, but she was a good sport and kept most of her angst to herself.

My next big venture was a garage sale at my friend Duane's house. Duane also lived in our neighborhood. Toby and I earnestly cleaned up our old Nintendo cartridges and anything else we could find and spent a lot of time pricing things. I had learned my lesson, though. We pooled our allowance money and bought an ad in the Seymour *Tribune*, and you know what? It worked. We sold a lot of stuff and I have to say, I was stoked. I loved the idea of trading toys and games I no longer wanted for money I could use to buy something I did want. What a concept!

I thought that each of our events turned out well for two main reasons. One, I had hardly spent anything on them, and two, I had learned something. My mission now, whether I realized it or not, was to take what I had learned and apply it to my relationships at school.

Every project, I also learned, every "business," has two components, income and expenses. Obviously the goal was for income to outweigh expenses and I quickly realized that didn't always happen.

■ ■ ■

AFTER MY SURGERY I was also trying very hard to fit into a school that had a lot of hormonal teenagers. At that age fitting in is everything. You want to walk alike, talk alike, style your hair the same way, and wear the same brand of clothing. None of that worked for me. Not even my clothes. Because our arms and legs were so short, Mom could never buy clothes off the rack for Toby or me. She had to make or alter everything Toby and I wore. Mom was a great seamstress and made us wonderful clothes, but it wasn't like I could share in the shopping experience at the mall with my friends.

Another issue in my quest to be just like everyone else was that I kept finding myself having crushes on girls. The problem was, no one was having crushes on me. In the seventh grade I liked a lot of girls. I guess you could say I was a "serial crush" kind of guy.

When I was six or seven years old Trinity Gossett was in my first communion class and apparently was smitten with me. One day my family and I were at my grandma and grandpa Wilson's house in Franklin, Indiana, when Mom began teasing me about Trinity and liking girls in general. I don't think some adults realize how embarrassed kids can get when it comes to the opposite sex.

The teasing more than mortified me and from then on I felt I had to hide my feelings not only from my parents, but also from my friends. The teasing made that much of an impact. My extreme embarrassment also caused me not to be able to discuss girl-related problems with my parents or to get advice on such matters from them.

I know now, as an adult, that the outcome of this scenario was very detrimental to me. I've discovered that once you bottle up your feelings that deeply, it is very hard to peel off the layers of the "onion" and let those feelings go. I truly believe that some of my problems as an adult with depression, drinking, gambling, and women had to do with my not being able to express my feelings when I was younger.

I can't tell you how much I wanted to have a girlfriend during these middle school years. It was all I thought about some days—okay, most days. While I always had girls who were friends, whenever I told them I had feelings for them we often drifted apart and were not friends anymore. With every girl, I'd get to the point where we talked and talked on the phone every night. I'd let my feelings build up until I couldn't stand it anymore, and boom. Each time that happened it was a devastating blow. I was crushed.

That happened over and over, and eventually taught me that rejection is a part of the game. I was so optimistic and willful that I was not afraid of rejection, so like a dog with a bone, I kept at it. Still, you can imagine how much unknown resentment this repeated rejection created within me. I was a nice guy. I was funny. I was fun. But I was also pretty headstrong at this time, not much different from my personality in early childhood. Looking back, I think some of the girls were less mature than I was and didn't want to deal with my strong personality, while others really did have issues with my dwarfism.

One day, to my intense joy, I learned that our school was going to have a dance. This was the first of what was going to be a series of dances and I could not wait! The school dance is a significant social rite and I was more than ready. But there was also a little anxiety mixed in with my joy. What would I wear? Could I dance? How would I dance? Would anyone even want to dance with me? I so desperately hoped someone would.

It turned out that even though I did not have a date for the dance, I had no shortage of partners. The girls I danced with were all confident, secure young women and we enjoyed each other's company as friends. You might wonder how, physically, I was able to dance. Well, I just stood up on my scooter and began to move. It worked out just fine and I had a lot of fun.

Of course, in middle school there was an actual school component. When I tried, I was a good student. Even though most of my teachers were quite good at teaching, rather than book work, I was far more interested in figuring out my newest business venture or seeing if Donna Rosetta or Lori Polley wanted to go to the next dance with me.

As you can tell, in many ways middle school was a frustrating time for me, and often there was a lot of angst, too. Rejection is rarely a happy event. But I have found that our experiences make us who we are. If I had not had those experiences I would not be who I am today, or where I am as a person—especially in my faith, which continues to grow by leaps and bounds.

■ ■ ■

WHEN I WAS fourteen another milestone was reached when Grandpa Wilson made me my first set of walking sticks and a box that allowed me to get on and off my scooter more easily. Both innovations nudged me toward independence and were precursors to the freedom I was yet to experience.

Because my back surgery reshaped my entire body, balance was an issue. My walking sticks are simply slim wooden dowel rods with a short dowel across the top. Heavy cloth straps attach to each side of the top cross dowel. My sticks come up to about my armpits. Rather than using the sticks as crutches, I grip them with my hands and use them more for balance and support. Since my fingers are so short, and with my middle knuckles fused, the design of the handles was especially important. Plus, I found I could use a walking stick as an extension of my arm to reach things, such as a salt shaker across a table, or to push away something I was through with.

These sound like minor actions, and to most people they are. But imagine having to crawl onto a table to reach a bottle of ketchup, or to continually have to ask someone else to get things for you. The walking sticks were brilliant in their simplicity and I use them every day, even now.

Grandpa Wilson's other innovation is a small wooden box on the floor of my scooter. Like the walking sticks, the box has a dual purpose. First, I can use the box as an aid to climb onto the scooter's seat. It still is a long reach for me from the floor of the scooter to the seat. Second, I can store things I need to carry with me there, such as books, papers, sunglasses, or my lunch. You name it, if it will fit into the scooter box, I've had it in there.

But my walking sticks and scooter box, as important as they were and are, were soon overshadowed by an idea that I had never considered. I thought if this idea actually became a reality, it would change my life forever. And it did.

I discovered this life-changing idea at a Little People of America meeting. My family and I had gone to our local chapter meetings quite regularly when I was younger. I fully believe in the idea that there are no coincidences. I believe that God puts opportunities into our lives and brings the people we need to us when we need them. That's how I feel about this particular meeting. I am so very glad we attended this time, for there I met a fellow dwarf named Greg Fehribach who not only had a van but drove it himself. When he let me sit in it, the wheels in my mind began turning. Prior to this meeting, the possibility that I would ever be able to drive was only a distant hope.

What a motivating eye-opener this chance encounter was for me. Because he was far less mobile than I, if he could drive, I knew I could too, and the world would be wide open to me. I could go to my friends' houses whenever I liked. I could take a girl out on a date. I could get a job and not have to worry about how I was going to get there. The thought of having my own van and driving it was absolutely electrifying and I immediately began thinking about how we could make that happen. It would take some time, but as you'll see, I got there.

■ ■ ■

THIS ALL LEADS me to a theory I have about the various stages of life. When you are four, you are the king of preschool, but when you enter kindergarten you drop back to the lowest member of the pack. Then, as you move up in rank, through second, third, and fourth grade, you once again rise to the top. As you rise, you feel more confident and in control. You have a voice, and wonder of all wonders, someone listens to it. Then you hit middle school and you once more drop down to the bottom rankings. This holds true, I believe, for every stage of your life, not only in school, but also in business and with family.

I've just recently come to understand this concept. Certainly in seventh grade I was nowhere close to making sense of it or even recognizing that such an idea existed. But that is exactly what happened. I went from being a confident, almost cocky, sixth grader to a bottom-of-the-barrel seventh grader, and as you have seen, I struggled a lot.

Much of what I struggled with was typical of any teenage boy, but I don't think any boy understands that. Each of us thinks he is the only one who goes through the upheaval of emotions and the awkward struggle with girls.

But most teenagers do not have the problems—the struggle with daily tasks, such as putting on shoes, dressing, or using the bathroom—that I do. My world was sure a roller coaster for those few years. Life was, however, going to get better. And soon. In high school, I not only had a ton of friends, I also found ways I could be a leader.

A PATH TO ACHIEVEMENT

Driving opened up an entirely new world for me, and it was a world of independence beyond my wildest dreams. Because of the enormous financial investment my driving would cost my parents it took a lot on my part to convince them that buying a van and having it modified would be an investment that paid many dividends.

The cost of putting me in a van was within my parents' ability but it was a stretch, because my parents only paid cash for things. We had a budget of thirteen thousand dollars for the van alone. It would be another thirteen thousand for the conversion, but if we waited two years until I was in college, we could get the conversion covered by a grant from the state of Indiana through their vocational rehabilitation program. I had to convince Mom and Dad that I needed the van *yesterday*.

I am very proud of the fact that even though I qualify for

multiple government assistance programs and services, the only times my parents or I have ever used those privileges are for the conversion of my second vehicle and for my scooters. This includes not taking one dime of Social Security or disability benefits, even though I am eligible. For the state of Indiana, it is a pretty good trade-off, keeping me mobile. With my modified vehicle and scooter I am able to earn a living and pay taxes, which means I do not have to rely on your tax dollars for my housing or living needs. This is said with absolutely no disrespect to those who genuinely need and utilize these services. I just knew that I was fortunate enough to be able to make do without them.

Me being the number cruncher that I am, I've figured that between Toby and me the state of Indiana has invested about one hundred thousand dollars in my vehicle modifications and scooters. But, between the two of us, we've paid more than 1.2 million in property taxes from our many ongoing ventures. That's about a 1,200 percent return on their investment. I am very proud that with my vehicle and scooter I am able to earn my own way and pay taxes instead of taking them.

I remember one day when I was in college I approached a girl with an obvious disability who was crying in the lobby of my dorm. I asked her what was wrong and she said she had put some birthday money into her bank account and that because she was on Social Security and was supposed to have a limited income, they had reduced her next check by that amount. I felt deep compassion for her, but in that moment I thought to myself, Wow, I'll never let our government, which is too big anyway, limit the amount of wealth I can create. I respect everyone's position in the matter, but this is mine.

■ ■ ■

WHEN IT CAME to the van, my main argument to my parents was that I if I had a modified vehicle I could drive Toby around, instead of Mom having to do so. In addition to being Toby's taxi, I could get a job, which I desperately wanted. I would then not have to rely on gift money or odd jobs for income.

Because Mom had been a teacher, higher education, productivity, and achievement were expected milestones in our household, and transportation was a big part of making all that happen. I am very thankful she thought that way.

Even though I knew we could find a used van that was sturdy enough for the modifications I required, my parents waffled about spending the money on it. I have mentioned that my dad was a good provider, and he was, but coughing up twenty-six thousand, plus funds for gas, insurance, and ongoing maintenance, was a huge commitment.

One night while eating dinner, which we always did as a family, I felt pushed over the edge. Since learning of the possibility of driving, my dreams had grown really big. During my teenage years, I had always dreamed of taking a girl on a date. But how could I accomplish that without my own transportation? I knew that over time it would cost far more than the price of the van and the conversion to hire someone to drive me around. I was so desperate and frustrated that I broke down in tears, pleading to my mom and dad, telling them if I were average size I'd drive a rusty old Volkswagen if it would allow me to drive like everyone else. After my masterful pitch, Mom and Dad agreed. I was so excited I could barely breathe!

A few things needed to happen before I could drive down the road in my own vehicle, though. The state required me to have a special physical and cognitive evaluation before I could enroll in driver's ed. The evaluation was needed because my unique physical circumstances required modifications to any vehicle that I drove. Before my parents spent the money for the van and before I took time for the class, we needed to be sure the state would eventually issue me a driver's license.

There was no doubt in my mind that I could drive, if I was given the opportunity and had the right equipment. However, I had a ton of anxiety leading up to the day of the evaluation because this was something I could not control, nor did I feel the evaluation was necessary. I had control over many things that tied into my being able to drive, such as the kind of van we needed to purchase and how well I prepared for the driving tests, but I feared the evaluators would suggest many more modifications than were actually necessary, which would cost my parents a lot more money.

If the evaluator suggested too many additional modifications it might scare my parents into holding off on the whole project. If this happened, even after my trials with my scoliosis surgery, it would be the biggest blow of my life up to that point.

Going into the evaluation, I was very positive about the day-long ordeal. I also realized that if I didn't cooperate fully, it could negatively affect the evaluator's opinion. I knew I needed to play the game and be into it as much as possible—tough to do when the results, either way, would be life-changing.

Once the evaluation began I felt more and more comfortable. Once I realized how easy the battery of mental and physical tests was, it was a piece of cake. I knew I was going to pass, which meant I knew I was going to drive! This was one of the points in my life when I realized I could do anything I put my mind to. For most of my life I was used to having to kick down doors; however, that day the doors to my future were flung wide open, and I was ready to stampede right through them.

■ ■ ■

SOON AFTER MY evaluation we saw an ad in the paper for a blue and white 1989 Ford van. It was a one-year-old Econoline 150 shorty model. This was the second thing that needed to happen. We had to find the right vehicle. While I really would have driven an old beater of a car if I was physically able, a van was ideal because it could have a lift added that would bring my motorized scooter up to the level of the floor of the van. And there was room for my scooter inside the van.

There was no way I, or even you, for that matter, could lift my scooter into an unmodified vehicle. I am on something like my twelfth scooter and each one of them has been far too heavy. Of course, other modifications would also be needed to accommodate my short arms and legs.

The asking price of the van was more than my parents wanted to pay, so we made an offer that was in line with the money they had set aside for this. We made the offer and I was on pins and needles waiting for a response; the wait felt like an eternity but was really only a week.

I remember exactly when and where I was when I learned we were going to purchase the van. There is an annual event in Jackson County, Indiana, called Fort Vallonia Days, where my dad went every year to shoot muzzle-loaders. Guns and flea markets were an interest that Dad and I had in common and there was also a giant flea market at the event. I had just gotten something to eat and was on my way to the shooting range to watch my dad shoot in the competition when I got a page from my mom. Back then I carried a pager and a cell phone, but I only used the cell phone for emergencies and to call out. My heart started pounding and I wondered if this was the moment we had been waiting for. And it was. Mom answered the phone and said, "Are you ready to start driver's ed?"

Long story short, the next day Mom and Dad purchased the van, and it was one of the happiest days of my life. Little did I know that it would then take a year for all the conversions to be done. That was definitely the longest year of my life.

Once I saw all that had been done to the van, I knew it had been worth the wait; however, I was still chomping at the bit. First, a drawbridge-style lift made by Braun had been installed. For many years the Braun company has set the standard in designing equipment for modifications like those being done to my van.

Next was a six-way power seat: up, down, back, forward, left, and right. The seat turned ninety degrees sideways so I could transfer easily from my scooter. It also had a thick back cushion that positioned me toward the front of the captain's chair and closer to the steering wheel.

The pedals, gearshift, and turn signals all had extensions so I could reach them. A very small steering wheel had been installed so my short arms and small hands could manage it. Other controls, such as the headlights, door locks, and power windows, were placed in a switch panel just below the window on the driver's-side door.

Finally, the middle seats were removed, leaving only the driver's and passenger seat in front and the bench seat along the back. This gave me lots of room to fit not only my scooter but also Toby's in the van. With this room I could slide easily from my scooter to the driver's seat. How cool was that? Me in the driver's seat!

The van was finally ready in October of my sixteenth year, and I was able to take driver's ed in my newly converted vehicle. The Ahnafield Corporation in Indianapolis facilitated all of the conversion and also added a brake on the passenger side, just like they had in the driver's ed cars at school.

Once I got my permit, Dad took time from work to help me build my driving skills, which I know was a big sacrifice, considering his workaholic tendencies. I think that most parents experience a mixture of fear and anxiety in teaching their children to drive, and sometimes it manifests as anger. I remember that once Dad got very upset with me for not coming to a complete stop at a yield sign. A yield sign? Come on. I knew I did not have to make a complete stop there. I was so mad I drove right home and showed him the rules that were printed in my driver's ed book. Having the ability to drive was so important to me that I not only knew every word that was printed in that book, I knew what page each word was on. Turns out that the particular yield sign my dad was upset about was next to a railroad track, so in a way, we were both right. But the incident showed him how seriously I took the responsibility of driving.

When it came time to take my driver's test I was more than ready. This was my last hurdle and it was, by far, the easiest. In fact, I aced both the written and the driving part of the test, and my only restriction was having to wear glasses. I was now a legal driver! I could drive by myself anywhere in the United States. Anywhere I wanted to go, anything I wanted to see, anything I wanted to do, I could.

You have to realize that for a person who could not dress himself, tie his shoes, or use the bathroom on his own, being able to drive was a *huge* jump forward toward independence. My mobility and independence are things I am extremely thankful for, and driving has been the biggest part of that. Plus, Mom realized that the van was one of the best investments she and my dad ever made, because she no longer had to shuttle Toby and me around.

It is important for me to also mention that unlike a formerly fully able-bodied person, such as an accident victim who now may be an amputee or a paraplegic, living in a very short body is all I know, and I am thankful for that. God chose this body for me, and I planned to use it in every way possible. Because I never had the experience of being "able-bodied" I didn't know or care what I was supposedly missing.

■ ■ ■

I HAVE MENTIONED that years earlier my parents made a conscious decision not to send me to kindergarten until I was six. My birthday is in July, so that meant I had a year more to mature and develop than most of my classmates when I started school. It also meant that I was the first of my friends do a lot of things that were age related, including, most importantly to me, driving. In my circle of friends, driving gave a huge boost to my popularity and leadership. All of a sudden I was the go-to guy for running to Wal-Mart or the record store, and I loved it.

I knew that my ability to drive was the cause of my new leadership position, but it didn't matter to me. I am still friends to this day with many of the kids that I bonded with through my van, and their friendship is a wonderful treasure I carry with me. I also realized that sometimes it doesn't matter *how* something happens, as long as it *happens*. If the van ended up being a tool that made me the "it" friend, so be it.

In addition to my van being the perfect vehicle for me, in more ways than one, my newly found status as designated driver meant I could now participate in some real teenage fun. And I have to say I took full advantage of it.

Honestly, during this time I got away with a lot of things I shouldn't have. In hindsight, people always gave me the benefit of the doubt when maybe they should have called me out on a few things. On more than one occasion I had a van full of kids hanging their heads and arms and legs out the windows, and even the back door.

There were a number of times that my friends and I almost got caught doing something we shouldn't have been doing, but one night sticks out in my mind, probably because I really was completely innocent. On this particular night Toby, my friend Bubba, some other friends, and I went to the Dairy Queen in my van. Unlike he is today, at that point in his life, Bubba was a big guy. I mean really big, three hundred fifty pounds or more. Back then Bubba was also a bit spoiled and inconsiderate.

At the Dairy Queen Bubba got a chocolate malt and, halfway back to his house, he decided he didn't want it, so he purposely threw it out the window at a truck that was parked in a residential driveway. After Bubba threw out the shake I heard a "Hey, you!" through my open window but, for whatever reason, we didn't stop to investigate. We all went to Bubba's house and got in his convertible to drive back past the scene. When we drove past, the people on the porch in front of the house again yelled at us to stop. Instead, we took off and enjoyed the rest of the evening cruising around town.

When Toby and I got home Dad was waiting.

"Why were you out egging cars?" he demanded.

I couldn't imagine what he was talking about. While I was often guilty of having fun, van surfing was more my style than egging cars. In fact, I don't think I ever did anything that was considered mean.

Dad then told me the police were called with my license plate number. The caller complained that whoever was driving that vehicle was out throwing eggs at cars. All of a sudden it hit me what had happened. I called the police myself and told them what was going on. The result was that Bubba had to go out at ten o'clock in the evening and wash the guy's truck.

Today Bubba is a very successful businessman and one of my best friends, but back then he was always a wild card. That may have been because he lost his father when he was thirteen. I should have learned something there about the kind of company you keep, but I didn't. I was still naïve enough to believe that the more friends I had the better, and it didn't matter who they were. It would take me an additional twenty years to figure out how wrong I was.

■ ■ ■

AS THE MONTHS wore on, my innocent cruising with up to nineteen kids in my van gave way to more serious "fun." And inadvertently, my dad opened the door to it all. A few years earlier, when I was fourteen or fifteen, my dad bought what we called "the farm." The farm was twelve acres just outside of town, and it had a house and several small barns and shacks on the property. Dad had a side business of digging swimming pools and sewers with his backhoe, and he also still had his dump truck.

The farm was purchased for several reasons. One, it served as a free source of fill dirt for Dad's projects. Two, Mom and Dad rented out the house and a few acres, so the land paid for itself. When I was about seventeen, my friends and I decided to turn the old hog barn on the farm into a hangout shack of sorts. We called it "the cabin."

We spent just about every day that summer caulking the old boards and fixing the leaky roof. One of my friends had a job at the local Ace Hardware and got us supplies at cost. The family of my brother's best friend, Toby Lawson, lived in the rental house and we ran a long electric cord from that house to the cabin. Toby L. knew how to help both of us to the bathroom so the three of us often hung out. There was already running water in the cabin and we hauled in carpet and an old college-dorm-sized refrigerator. We also dug a fire pit. It was then party time!

Our parties started off pretty innocently, as these things often do, but it wasn't long before we began experimenting with alcohol. Someone's sister was twenty-one, and she supplied us with beer and vodka. One thing led to another and before we knew it, we were having regular weekend cabin parties.

Our one big rule was that at each party we had a designated person to clean up all the "evidence" and take it with them to dispose of somewhere. One weekend that didn't happen and my mom woke me up on a Saturday morning. She asked if I knew anything about beer being at the cabin the night before.

"Wow," I said with fake surprise. "Someone must have broken in and had a party."

I felt so bad lying to her. I never knew if Mom believed me or not, but I didn't want my friends to get into trouble or our cabin privileges to be revoked. This was the first time alcohol could have gotten me into trouble, but it certainly wasn't the last. Another time the mother of a girl who was at one of our parties called me and threatened to call my dad and ask him if he knew what was going on at the cabin. This phone call from a friend's mother scared me to death, but Dad was, and is, a pretty easygoing guy. In fact, I think he knew what was going on at the cabin.

I was pretty hardheaded and if my dad had not allowed me a little leeway I think I would have rebelled strongly. We were mischievous, but we weren't out of control—that came in my twenties. Having my own vehicle was a whole lot more fun than my friends and I throwing shucked corn kernels at the neighbors' windows on Halloween (which is called "corning"). No one ever said anything then, either, and we again got away with more than we should have. I didn't realize until much later that my scooter tracks in the yards around my neighborhood gave me away!

Still, I felt like I was on top of the world. Being the first of my friends to have a car, and suddenly becoming popular, made me feel like the king of the kingdom.

Unfortunately, my leading of the kingdom was about to come to a quick demise. My friend Duane was the next of my friends to turn sixteen, and when he got his license that took some of my power away. Other kids soon followed Duane and before I knew it, almost every kid in my class had a license.

I still had lots of friends; I was still having fun. But it wasn't quite the same. I loved being a leader. Driving made me believe that anything was possible. I also realized that entitlement has no part in leadership, possibility, or opportunity. Hard work does, and I had worked ten times as hard to get my license as most other kids. I understood on a new level that success is not just a matter of dreaming to achieve a goal; there are and continue to be countless dreams. Success was a matter of putting in the time and focus to achieve your dreams.

Of course during this time there was also school. Back in the sixth grade we all took a test that divided us into levels. Level-one students were advanced, level twos were considered in the "normal" range, and level threes were "slower" learners.

I had been placed mostly in level-two classes in middle school but also had some level-one English and science classes. I didn't realize it then, but those levels created a social class that would carry us into high school and far beyond. It segmented us and fractured us into groups where expectations were fixed.

As a result, I had a middle school math teacher who did not expect much of me, and you know what? I ended up delivering as little as possible. In that way, I absolutely met all of his expectations. I wish we could find an education system that challenged each and every student to reach deep within and surpass all expectations and boundaries. I was fortunate in high school to have a math teacher who did just that.

I was at least one grade level behind in math when I entered high school, but Miss Hart pushed and prodded me to excellence. I hated her at the time, but she was a teacher who knew she was not there to be liked. She was the kind of teacher who was a rigid disciplinarian and who often gave pop quizzes. She also expected us to be able to rattle off any number of multiplication tables and know our square roots.

Miss Hart was there to teach, and she did, but I didn't make it easy for her. I was a smart-aleck kid who always asked her why we needed to know a specific skill. No thanks to me, she got me caught up and I owe a lot of my business acumen to her. In her class I even learned to work a few chapters ahead so I'd be prepared. Because of her I can develop my own spreadsheets and understand the financial aspects of a business plan. I can look at a business deal and figure out better ways to create win-win scenarios for both parties. In fact, about the only thing having to do with finances that I don't do for all my businesses now is my taxes.

It really is amazing that it only took one teacher who removed all low expectations, all boundaries, for me to achieve. I learned so much more than math from her, and I now look at everyone I meet as a blank slate of infinite possibilities. Even better, I feel the same way about me.

THINKING OUTSIDE
THE BOX: WHAT BOX?

The summer I was seventeen, on a rather average day, I drove Toby to his girlfriend's house and dropped him off. On the way back, I realized I had to use the bathroom, badly, but even if I found a bathroom, there was no one available to help me use it, especially since I had to go "number two." With the exception of a few friends and family members, Mom was still the only one who could help me use the bathroom. So I rushed home, squirming all the way with a mounting fear that I'd poop in my pants and all over my van before I got there.

I experienced an incredible sense of urgency. I parked in the driveway and made it out of my van to find it was one of the rare times that Mom was not home. Although I made it out of my van, immediately after, I pooped in my pants. Big-time. I was so embarrassed and helpless and frustrated and mad that I wanted to cry. I was wearing shorts and my mess was running down the backs of my legs and into my shoes. Here I was seventeen years old and I still could not use the bathroom by myself. Talk about a depressing realization.

I didn't have a key to the house, and even if I had, I could not have reached the doorknob. So, sitting on the edge of the wheel of my go-kart, I waited outside for Mom to get home. When she did, she was not happy. After all, she and I had trained my bowels to move at certain times of the day, and this was not one of them. On that day I felt each and every one of Mom's emotions on top of all of mine. It was quite a load, no pun intended.

Since that day I have learned to do a lot more for myself, including using the bathroom (and I'll explain how later).

This is probably as good a time as any to mention some of those tasks because they are such a big part of my day and probably are so very different from the way you do things. I live in a world where different is not better or worse, it is just different. But I have found that people are often uncomfortable with difference—until they understand it. I am jumping ahead a little here, but in doing so you will better understand the special challenges of my high school years and beyond.

I know that most people, when they see me for the first time, have an automatic response of feeling sorry for me. I see it on their faces, in their body language. I've seen this instinctive reaction in others all my life, and I wish they would stop to consider *me* first, before they judge my body.

I am blessed to have so much opportunity in my life; it really is beyond belief. I own multiple businesses, am enriched with hundreds—even thousands—of friends. I travel across the country entertaining thousands of people a night and am privileged to know some of the most influential people of our day. Not everyone can say that and I never forget how lucky I am.

It is interesting to me that while adults are sometimes uncomfortable with me at first, kids are just the opposite. Kids are intrigued. Little kids especially are hyperaware of me and I don't know if that is because they are so much more aware of their surroundings than adults are or if it has to do with my small size.

Kids also open up to me and accept me far more easily than most adults do. They are curious about me, my scooter, and how I do things. Kids have no filter and if they have a question, they'll ask.

In contrast, adults tend to pretend I am not there, or they might give me a cursory glance and then look away. That is, unless they recognize me from Big & Rich concerts, where I am the Ambassador of Attractions. As Ambassador of Attractions I get the crowd riled up before Big & Rich concerts, introduce the acts, dance onstage to some of the songs, and interact with all of the fans. People might also recognize me from my appearances on national television shows, such as *The Celebrity Apprentice*. Then adults become as open as kids do.

It's the recognition factor that changes everything for adults, and to me, recognition means education. Once someone knows who I am, they know I am a friendly guy who has never met a stranger. Dwarfism aside, my openness is genuine. It's part of my personality, but I have found that it also puts people at ease and minimizes the differences between us.

So what are some of the differences? There are many, so I'll touch on a few of the ones that would be the most visible to you or that impact my day the most. One difference is that while you might hold a glass or a cup with one hand, I use two. My fingers are short and my hands are small, so I need the grip and balance and leverage of both of my hands to use a cup.

I mentioned leverage, and that is a big part of my world. It is in yours, too, but you probably are not as aware of it. Leverage is an important thing to have in every part of your life, from business to relationships, but it is also important in the physical realm. Here's what I mean: to do something, such as get up out of a chair, you might push, but I pull. It is all leverage, but everyone uses it in different ways. Because my legs are substantially disproportionate I often pull with my arms, rather than push with my feet, as you might do.

In carrying an object (let's say a notebook), you might grasp it in your hand and then place it on a table, while I will carry it in the crook of my elbow and then leverage it onto a flat surface with a twist of my chest and arm. The result is the same; it's just the process of getting there that differs.

Because I use my sticks to walk short distances, my upper body is strong. I do push-ups and walk on a treadmill at the YMCA. Almost any machine at the YMCA that I want to use, I adapt. For example, with the treadmill, I bring ropes with me that wrap around the handle that controls the on/off switch and the speed. Then I pull on a rope to adjust the speed or turn the machine off. Jogging or running is the only kind of exercise I can't modify enough to do at all. And I technically could do something such as ski, just to prove I could do it, but I'm pretty sure my body wouldn't hold up if I skied regularly.

Most people would carry a backpack or a satchel, but because a backpack makes me top-heavy and unbalanced I carry things I need with me—like pens, pencils, a notepad, medicine, breath mints, sunglasses—in a small Ziploc plastic bag tucked in my scooter box. That way I have no fear that they will spill out or that I won't be able to find them. Organization is a necessary part of the territory of dwarfism.

A lot of guys keep their wallet in their pants pocket, but with my short arms that is not an easy area for me to reach. Instead, you will typically see me with a wallet hanging from a shower curtain hook on the handlebars of my scooter. I also often wear a T-shirt with a breast pocket and if I am away from my scooter, that's where I carry my wallet.

I also write differently than most people do. While most people use one hand, I use two. I am forever grateful to my early teachers who allowed me room to figure out the best way for me to do some of the most basic daily tasks, such as writing. My right hand is dominant, but I need my left hand for balance and leverage. I also often stand on a chair that is next to a table to write, rather than sit on the chair. Sitting does not give me enough clearance in height, nor does it put me at the right angle to put pencil to paper successfully.

When I was younger I wrote things by hand a lot more than I do now. That's true of most adults, I believe. We all did more writing by hand when we were in school. Because a standard-sized pencil was so long for me, throughout school I often had an eraser smudge mark on the right side of my neck from using it for leverage. Writing with a short pencil was not an option because it did not give me enough room to hold it in both of my hands. Sometimes you just have to compromise.

It is so important for anyone with some sort of difference, whether physical, cognitive, or emotional, to be able to find out what works for them, and also for those around that person to value and support whichever unique method works. Who cares how the writing is accomplished, as long as it is?

Eating also presents challenges for me, especially due to my short fingers and fused joints. Somehow, I learned to thread the handle of a fork or a spoon through the fingers of my right hand. In this way, with the handle above my index and pinky fingers, and below my middle and ring fingers, I get enough leverage and stability to bring food to my mouth. You only have to look at me to know that I am not anywhere close to starving myself!

More recently I have begun wearing rings, but I found I have to take them off before I eat, or it interferes with how I hold the fork or spoon. I then have to remember to put them back on again, especially if I am at a restaurant.

How I get food and beverages open is another matter. It is a good thing that I have strong teeth, because I use them for a lot more than chewing. From opening packages and bottle tops to opening CD cases or the battery compartment of my phone, I generally use my teeth. I don't use my fingernails or fist because it is a leverage issue. I can't curl my fingers or have enough grip. Using my teeth is an effective way for me to do something quickly that otherwise I would have to ask someone else to do. My independence and mobility mean so much to me; I will gladly use my teeth to achieve that.

As far as cooking, I never use a stove. In fact, I even moved my stove out of my apartment and put it in one of my business offices. I do not have enough strength or leverage or stability to make cooking over a hot stove a safe activity. But I do use a microwave or sometimes a toaster oven. I eat out regularly and snack on granola bars, and sometimes bananas.

At this point in my life I try to eat as healthily as possible, although you will soon see that was not always the case. I'm big on food products without preservatives and I take a lot of vitamins and supplements, so I am not worried that nutritionally I am missing something due to my lack of stove skills.

Earlier I mentioned my walking sticks and I use them a lot to leverage myself. I might slide sideways from a chair onto my scooter seat and then leverage a turn with one of my sticks so I am facing forward.

Bathing and dressing present another set of challenges. To bathe, I need a shower with a very low lip so I can get in and out safely. Crawling into and out of a regular bathtub, especially when it is wet, is pretty dangerous for me to attempt, even when using my sticks. The faucets also need to be low, so I can reach them.

In dressing, I know that I can spend a lot of time getting ready for the day. I have a set of sticks with brass hooks on the end that I run through my pants legs and hook the hems. Then I can pull my pants on. I do the same for putting on my socks. Think of the sticks as arm extensions. Fortunately, I still have dozens of sets of sticks that my grandpa made, with different hooks and handles on them. Some have handles and no straps. I am so thankful that Grandpa was able to think far enough outside the box to anticipate all of my needs and design the various sets of sticks accordingly.

When it comes to shoes, I used to wear shoes with zippers in them instead of loafers or laces. My clubfeet do not fit well into a loafer-style shoe. I need something with more support so Mom figured out a way to insert zippers in the shoes Toby and I wore when we were younger. Now I wear shoes with speed laces. These are the elastic kind of laces you often see runners wear. Just pull the laces and they tighten right up. I am ready to go. The only difficulty I sometimes have now with my shoes is getting the tongue pulled up just right before I tighten the laces. My sticks also help me pull the shoe tongue up.

As you might imagine, I am always aware of my physical surroundings, including curbs and steps, bathrooms, and entrances to public places, such as restaurants and businesses. My subconscious has integrated my need to find physical access to places so thoroughly that I am no longer aware that I am doing it. It is just part of my life, just as grabbing your keys as you walk out the door in the morning might be part of your life. At the same time, I recognize that this is something other people rarely think about. There's a door; in you go. That is not always true for me, however, because my scooter can't go up or down a series of steps and I cannot open most doors by myself unless they are power operated.

In the past, many friends and acquaintances have accused me of being bossy or controlling. When that happens I try to explain that I am not being controlling when I prefer one restaurant or one table over another. It simply is a matter of my thinking ahead and being aware of my surroundings in any given situation. If I might need to use the bathroom, for example, I always think ahead about how my scooter will fit through the door, how the bathroom is set up, and what assistance I might need. How will I get from point A to point B?

That level of preparedness also flows so innately into my work situations, and also into my personal relationships, that I sometimes do not think about it when I should. In these situations I do not have to be so controlling, but it is such a habit of self-preservation that it is hard for me to let go and trust that someone else will choose well on my behalf. Believe me, I have done a lot of inward thinking to get to this point and there's still plenty of room to grow.

Also, the entire time I was writing this book I was incessantly late to my writing sessions with my coauthor, the very patient Lisa Wysocky. There is no excuse, but rather a reason for my tardiness. One reason truly is procrastination. The other is because of my unique physical challenges.

I was late one day, for example, because I had to pack for an ESPN shoot. Two of my bags got hooked together when I used a precarious, but adaptive, way to lift them onto my scooter. It took me twenty minutes to untangle them, while it would have taken an able-bodied person two minutes. I'm not saying this to complain, I just want to give you a view into my world. I also think that if the worst part of my day is to spend twenty minutes unhooking two bags that are clipped together, then I am in pretty good shape.

As you can see, there are a lot of differences between you and me. But we are also much the same. I have the same desire to live a comfortable life, have professional and creative success, and have a family as you probably do. I want to support my friends, help other people, and deepen my relationship with my lord and savior. I want to be a good son and brother, nephew and cousin. So in those ways, the ways that count, we are not so different after all.

■ ■ ■

AS YOU MIGHT guess, I had to be creative in my interactions with friends and classmates as I was a typical teen but had a body that was different from theirs. One thing I found was that it was hard to be open with friends about perceived differences, and educating them was often a matter of trial and error. Many of those educational experiences, from my side and theirs, came from hanging out together. This was especially difficult when it came to any possible relationship with friends who happened to be girls. While I couldn't articulate any of that with girls then, I have no problem with it now. I also found my lack of openness a barrier between girls I liked and me, and I wish I could have had open conversations about how they felt about my short stature.

For me it was never fast enough or far enough. While I eventually became more comfortable with the opposite sex, I was never able to find the elusive girlfriend of my dreams. My girl friends preferred to stay just that: girls who were friends, and nothing more.

While I thought about that a lot, sometimes obsessively, I was also in high school now and had a lot going on. I was about to become an Eagle Scout, the Boy Scouts' top rank. I also had several businesses to start and a college selection to make. Time to get busy.

9

REALIZING MY POTENTIAL

In high school I became more involved in business ventures. I'd known for some time that I wanted to own my own businesses, many of them, and now my mind was always turning with ideas. I had lots of what I thought were great ideas and you know, some of them actually were. However, there were a few ideas that never quite made it off the ground. Some of those I am still tweaking, so they may see the light of day at some point. Others, well, all I can say is that they showed interesting creativity.

One day when I was a freshman, which was ninth grade in the Seymour school system, out of the blue a kid at school offered me a quarter for a piece of Bubblicious gum. We weren't supposed to have any gum or candy at school, but I always managed to have a few pieces tucked away in my pencil bag. My brain whirled into action and I realized if I sold each piece of gum in the five-piece pack for a quarter, I'd make a dollar and twenty-five cents a pack. Selling several packs a day was big money for a ninth grader in the late 1980s. Plus, I got my mom to buy the gum for me so I had no overhead. Income with no expenses—are you kidding me?

A little later I was staying at Aunt Linda's house while Toby had back surgery and she wondered how in the world I was going through so much gum. At first I thought she was going to be mad when I told her, but it turned out that she was relieved that I wasn't chewing it all. By this time I was selling a lot of gum. Word had spread and I had a fairly large clientele, including a number of girls whom I got to become friends with. In that way, my early business ventures prepped me for making money, and more importantly, meeting girls.

Later I expanded my "store" to include candy and other kinds of gum. I was thrilled with the pocket change I was earning, and also with the new faces who were quickly turning into friends. I loved being the "candy man." I'd make fifteen or twenty dollars a week in profit, along with a helpful amount of confidence.

■ ■ ■

IN ADDITION TO my business interests I was adjusting to a new school. While Seymour Middle School had been housed in one single-story newer building, Seymour High School was an older building on two levels with a newer annex building. This meant rather than scootering from one class to the next with my friends, I used the small, creaky elevator and went outside even in the most extreme hot and cold temperatures to get to the annex.

I remember one accounting class that I had in high school. It was upstairs in the main building and one day the thermometer in class read one hundred ten degrees. This was even with the windows open and fans blowing. This particular teacher didn't want us to have water in class, and the result was a bunch of hot, grumpy, unfocused kids.

A lot of people love warm temperatures, but I normally am very hot anyway. That might be because of my shortened limbs, or it might just be how I am wired. Long story short, I didn't get sick, but the discomfort of that day remains imprinted in my mind as one of my less productive days of high school. Hopefully today, school districts will not allow that to happen. There is no way a kid can learn anything in that kind of environment.

Environmental issues aside, my high school years were the last years I felt truly safe in the world. I still had a lot of naïvety for my age and did not understand that as an adult, life often gets in the way of your dreams. Relationship troubles, problems with money, important moral and ethical decisions, addiction, physical abuse—all of those were foreign concepts to me. I didn't understand those kinds of troubles at all and blissfully went about in my own safe little world. I know now that God was watching over me, protecting me, giving me more time to mature. Of course, many of my future problems would be of my own making, but for now, I was thrilled to be a businessman.

One of the first businesses I started in high school was a DJ service with my friend Duane. We were freshmen then and played CDs and cassette singles at high school dances. We started by putting our two home stereo systems together. Duane moved equipment and took care of the technical stuff, and I was the front man at the events and also took care of the business side.

Eventually Duane wanted out, and Grandpa Wilson loaned me a thousand dollars to upgrade the equipment. We had been doing middle school dances, but with the new equipment I added high school events. I charged sixty dollars an hour and really did quite well, plus I had not spent much, if anything, from all of my earlier business ventures.

I hired a kid from down the street, Brian Lee, to move equipment for me, and my old friend David McKain helped as well. That worked out just fine, but one day I had a brilliant idea. Rather than be a hired gun at these events, I could stage my own. Why be limited to sixty dollars an hour, less overhead? I could rent a hall and keep all the profit.

I first rented out the local Girls Club gym for high school dances after football and basketball games when there was no dance at the school. Because that went so well, I started thinking much bigger and recruited Jason McDaniel for a big, *big* event at the Indiana National Guard armory. I got my parents and all my aunts and uncles and cousins involved as chaperones. I have to say that I had a great deal of anxiety about whether or not people would come, but they did. In that area the event was a huge success. But not so much financially. When we tallied up all the overhead and expenses, Jason and I about broke even.

I also joined our high school business club and led an effort to reopen our school bookstore. I am happy to say that we were very successful. A bunch of us chipped in, and our accounting teacher went to the big-box store Sam's Club and bought notebooks, pens, paper, pencils, and other supplies. Each of us volunteered to take shifts to man the store. I learned so much during that time about price points, cost of goods, and customer service. At the end of the year we all cashed out and I had made a total of two hundred twenty-five dollars on a hundred-dollar investment. To you fellow number crunchers, that's 125 percent return on an investment. Pretty good, if I do say so myself. That was a lot of money for me at the time and it both fueled and validated my desire to learn more about business.

■ ■ ■

TO MAXIMIZE MY time, I used my study hall in school to actually study and do the homework I didn't want to do at home. A lot of other kids wasted that time, but I had things to do. At home, I remember my dad helping me with some of my vocabulary and English homework. To this day I do not know where he got the knowledge to diagram sentences properly but he had a real knack for it. I also don't know how he found the time to help me, but I am grateful. English was a strength of mine all through school and I was always placed in the highest classes; however, I abhorred biology and other science classes.

You can probably tell that I was not a straight-A student, although I think I could have been if I had given my studies my full attention. As I progressed in high school, my grades improved, not because I studied more, but because I became more focused on getting into college.

One thing I was especially interested in was SADD (Students Against Drunk Driving). I was very active in the organization and even helped design a float we had in a local parade. I fully believed in the SADD message. Actually, I still do. However, I now find it ironic that not too many years after I graduated I became one of those drunk drivers I warned everyone about when I was a student. Drinking was to become one of my life's biggest challenges. But at this point in my life my biggest trouble did not have to do with drinking or with school. It had to do with girls, and one girl in particular whom I was infatuated with.

Her name was Kayla Fechter. We had a couple of classes together, and once in a while I'd get up the nerve to ask her out. Kayla always had a reason to decline. She'd say, "Yes, but . . . ," and the "but" ranged from having to work, study, or go somewhere with her parents to attending a family gathering. Being naïve, I kept asking. Finally, I called my friend Duane, who worked at the same grocery store as Kayla, to see if he could find out what her work schedule was so I would know when to ask her to go out.

Duane said he would but never realized that after we were done speaking he didn't hang up the phone properly. I could hear him laughing away on the other end of the line. When his mom asked what was so funny, I also heard him tell her of my request and, in his mind, how ridiculous it was. To this day, even though we went on to become roommates in college, Duane does not know I heard all of that. Well, I guess he knows now.

The moment I heard Duane laughing, a big, hollow pit formed in the center of my stomach, but I quickly shooed it away and buried it. I would not realize for many years the effect hiding that emotion had on my inner self. I felt betrayed, humiliated, and angry all at the same time. I later found out that Duane also had feelings for Kayla, and years after we were all out of high school Kayla told me that another "friend" of mine talked her out of going out with me. If she *had* gone out with me, it would have changed my life. Since then I've had to give up a lot of resentment toward Duane and I did that by realizing that we were kids and kids do not always handle situations well. I have to say I realize now that Duane was too immature to understand at the time what he had done.

■　■　■

TOWARD THE END of my high school years I fulfilled a lifelong dream and became an Eagle Scout. Only 4 percent of Boy Scouts reach this rank and in achieving this milestone I joined a brotherhood of achievers. But it almost didn't happen.

If a Scout is going to get his Eagle, he must do so before his eighteenth birthday. I ended up having to scramble to make that happen. While I had been a dedicated Scout in my early teens, after I got my driver's license I became distracted by girls and cars and neglected some of my Scout duties. Fortunately, I got back on track in time, but it was only due to constant nudging from my Scout leaders, Ron Nelson and Mr. Norea.

My dad also played a part in this. He had achieved the rank of Life Scout, which is the rank just below Eagle. He told me many times that not getting his Eagle was one of the biggest regrets of his life. Thank goodness his message sank in.

Every prospective Eagle Scout has to complete a community service project, and I chose to plant several dozen trees around a local softball field called Freeman Field. Freeman Field is now an industrial facility with a recreation area and is maintained by the city of Seymour, but during World War II it was an air force base. The trees I got donated were pretty big, three to four feet tall, so I was not involved in a hands-on way with digging the holes and putting the trees in the ground, but I coordinated the entire project, from lining up the trees, volunteers, and digging equipment to arranging for the okay to plant there and planning the time and day. I am proud to say that those trees are still there and have all grown quite big. It was nice to be a catalyst in something that has had such long-lasting value to so many people.

I got a lot out of Scouting but realize it is not for everyone. In fact, my own brother was totally uninterested. However, if you have a son who shows some interest, I hope you wholeheartedly encourage him. He will learn so much about people and life that he cannot learn anywhere else. I'd also encourage you to put him on a track to obtain his Eagle rank before he starts to drive. In fact, if I ever have a son, if he is interested in Scouting, I am going to make getting his Eagle a requirement before he can get his driver's license. That's how strongly I feel about the program. I still live by the Scout motto, which is "Always Be Prepared," and it has served me very well.

■　■　■

JUST ABOUT EVERY summer our family took a trip with Grandma and Grandpa Wilson to Wisconsin. Grandma and Grandpa had vacationed in the same cabin on South Two Lake (aside from a few years spent at another cabin on Fawn Lake) in Oneida County every summer for more than fifty years. In fact, they were in Wisconsin when I was born. As I was born in July, we were always there during my birthday and it was a lot of fun.

Grandpa was a great fisherman and he taught both Toby and me to cast when we were very young. In fact, my dad said I could consistently hit a rubber tire at thirty feet by the time I was ten. During the day we'd fish for bluegill and occasionally go with Dad and Grandpa to fish for northern pike. At night we'd fish for largemouth bass. Dad and Grandpa cleaned the fish together and Grandpa fried everything we brought home.

A few years in, we realized that Grandpa used the same cooking oil over and over every year. We left a handful of things in a storage shed on the property from year to year and the used cooking oil was apparently one of those things. It is amazing that we didn't all get sick.

While these vacations were wonderful bonding trips for our family, traveling to one of them almost caused me serious harm. When I was about seventeen, we stopped on the way for gas. During the stop, I ran my scooter down a curb cut and right into the path of a parked truck that was about to move. I didn't realize there were people in the truck and that they were leaving instead of just parking. That error could have cost me my life. Fortunately, Dad was just behind me and let out a big yell and the driver stopped. The only thing that had an impact with the truck was the left armrest of my scooter.

Dad lectured me quite hard for an hour after that. "Do you want to get run over?" he asked over and over again. Of course I know now that his fear was manifesting as anger, but I didn't realize it at the time. What I did realize, maybe for the very first time, was how fragile life was. Now I can look back and understand that God must have seen that I needed a lesson in caution.

■ ■ ■

IN THE MIDST of all of this, I was trying to finalize my college plans. There never was any question about whether or not I would go to college. I always knew I would. Mom has a master's in education, and while Dad sacrificed college when he was drafted into the army, he fully supported the idea of higher education. I am really proud of my dad's service to our country. He was stationed in Germany and in Rome, Italy, in the sixties and helped guard the Nike Hercules missile sites. These were combat-ready missile-launch sites and he served smack in the middle of the Vietnam War.

I had been looking at various colleges based on their campus accessibility, including the University of Illinois, the University of Indiana, and Ball State University. Because of Ball State's Entrepreneurship Program, which was nationally ranked, I had decided on them before I ever set foot on campus.

Dr. Donald F. Kuratko, an amazing educator, founded and led this renowned program. Dr. K is dynamic, positive, open, and magnetic, and he alone sealed the deal for me. I couldn't wait to study under him! He is still considered one of the nation's premier educators in the field of entrepreneurship and now leads Indiana University's Kelley School of Business Entrepreneurship Program and holds the Jack M. Gill chair there (no relation to my Gill family).

The BSU campus really was an early leader in disabled accessibility. From curb cuts on every corner to tons of elevators and power doors, I felt certain I could navigate the campus with ease. And two hours away was close enough to home that I could drive back to Seymour whenever I needed to.

The fall of my senior year in high school, Duane and I drove to Muncie, Indiana, to visit the campus for Fall Preview Day. You might ask how I could remain friends with Duane after hearing him so rudely laugh off my idea about asking Kayla out. I'm not even certain myself, other than we had been friends for a long time. Some friendships can withstand a lot of upheaval and some can't. In many ways friendships are like marriages in that the partnerships are not always fifty-fifty.

Additionally, I needed Duane for physical assistance and a lot of our friendship was built on that. This was not a conscious thing, but it was an underlying factor as to why I remained friends with him. I also believe that on some level Duane may have needed me to cover up his own insecurities.

That's how my friendship was with Duane. I still touch base with him from time to time on Facebook. Duane has also never hesitated to ask me for concert tickets if someone I know is performing, but his requests have been met with the same response that he showed me over the phone, so it has come full circle.

Rooming with Duane aside, I loved what I saw at Ball State and was impressed with everyone I met. From then on, high school was a means to an end. To get to Ball State I had to cross a stage and pick up my high school diploma. I couldn't wait for that day to arrive, but finally it did.

Mom did a great job altering my graduation gown and I was

thrilled to put it on. A year or so before, Jacob Baker, a friend of mine with muscular dystrophy, had graduated from our high school. To accommodate his wheelchair the school built a ramp to the stage. This year my scooter and I would use that same ramp to pick up my diploma.

I admit that my excitement got the better of me, though. Principal John McCormack and Assistant Principal John Fee had been strong supporters of mine throughout high school. In fact, Mr. Fee had been my go-to guy for anything that I needed, and he had been great. During graduation, I thanked Mr. McCormack but forgot Mr. Fee, and I have felt badly about that ever since. I hope he reads this and accepts my belated gratitude.

High school was not any more of a horrible time for me than for anyone else, but I was so eager to leave it behind because I could not wait to start this newest leg of my life. I didn't know it then, but four years later I would feel exactly the same way when I graduated from college. In the meantime, however, I had a lot of living and learning to do. I was more than ready—so I thought.

LIFE DURING COLLEGE

While I was excited about going to college, I also had a lot of anxiety about my living scenario. Over the years I had become more and more independent, but I still could not use the bathroom by myself. As you can imagine, this was a never-ending source of deep frustration for me. For one, I had to be two steps ahead of everyone else. Did I have to go to the bathroom before my roommate left? Like a trip to the dentist, you know you have to go, but you still have bad anxiety about it. The difference is you typically become anxious about going to the dentist once or twice a year. I had to use the bathroom several times every day. I also needed help dressing and bathing, both of which most of you take for granted. Who would assist me when I needed help with these intimate tasks? I was in a regular state of anxiety, compounded by irritation and annoyance that I could not do these things for myself.

I was also a little surprised that I had more than a few misgivings about leaving Toby. Despite our differences in personality and interests, I had grown into the role of big brother well. I worried that without me around to show him the ropes of life he would lose his way. I needn't have worried; Toby managed to survive high school just fine without me.

Duane roomed with me, and that relieved some of my fear. I also had an attendant who came mornings and evenings to help me bathe, dress, and undress. That way I did not have to rely 100 percent on Duane. After all, he had his own classes and schedule to keep, which didn't always mesh with mine, and I knew deep down that he was much less concerned with his duties to me than I was.

I first met Milo, my attendant, the summer after my high school graduation. Mom, Dad, and I drove to Muncie to meet with him and he seemed capable enough that I felt comfortable with the thought of his helping me with bathroom doings, dressing and undressing, and showering. Milo was a married guy of about twenty-five who was working on a grad degree. In the meantime he was able to scratch his golf itch by working part-time in a golf shop.

Duane and I were assigned to Williams Hall in the Noyer complex of residence halls, two guys' dorms and two girls' dorms connected to a communal lobby and cafeteria. We quickly bonded with a group of guys who lived on our floor, the first, and also with some girls who lived in another part of the complex. This group and I hung out all the time. We went to the dollar cinema every Tuesday night, no matter what was playing. It was an eight-plex theater, so there was always something good. We also played euchre (a two-on-two team card game) and ate a ton of Papa John's pizza.

Papa John Schnatter and his brother Chuck both happen to be Ball State alumni. Later on, through mentoring I did with the Entrepreneurship Program, I met and became friends with Chuck. I also met John Schnatter at a NASCAR drivers' meeting, which most people never have the opportunity to go to, so it was another full circle scenario.

It was good that I made a number of friends quickly, in case I needed assistance in navigating the unfamiliar campus and with day-to-day living. Even with Milo and Duane to help, I sometimes needed assistance navigating my new environment or needed people to help carry a cafeteria tray or organize books in my scooter box.

Rich Harris, the director of disabled student services, gave me keys to elevators and special access to buildings via a credit card type of key that automatically opened outside doors. That helped a lot. The dorm room I lived in also had a private bath, and I had special parking privileges close to some of the buildings.

As happened in high school, my van and parking spot brought a lot of new friends to me really fast. Before my first month as a student was over I probably knew more people on campus than any other freshman. Not only did this network of friends help me then, it helps me today. If I need to know something, for example, about printing or banking or psychiatry, all I have to do is ask one of my friends who specialize in that area. In many ways I am only one degree away from anything and anybody I'll ever need to know. You can never know too many people, and I knew even then that no life goal or plan would move forward without an extensive network of personal and business relationships. This has little to do with my dwarfism. Instead, I believe it should be common sense for anyone who wants to fulfill a lifelong dream.

I have to say that I did not excel my first two semesters in college. I was taking mostly core requirement classes and, frankly, I was bored. So instead of studying or partying (too hard) I fell in love. Well, it really was more of a series of crushes.

A guy who lived down the hall introduced me to a girl named Kristi Grinstead and he later ended up dating her. But although he dated her, I fell in love with her. She was my first "love" in college. Then there were Jennifer Racine and Barb Terlap . . . among others. With each new crush I repeated the pattern I had established in high school. We became friends, but shortly after I declared my feelings, it was made clear to me that friends were all we were going to be. Despite that scenario, I was ever hopeful. I really am a hopeless romantic.

After a while I began giving girls neck messages in the dorm common areas, where we hung out most of the time. That was a way I could be "intimate" with a girl. It wasn't the same as the relationship that I desired so badly, but it was better than nothing. Plus, I got pretty good at it and it has since served me very well.

One evening I was in the bathroom brushing my teeth when I began voicing my frustrations to Milo about a girl I had recently met. I really liked her but had been told we needed to remain friends. Milo casually practiced a golf swing in the reflection of the full-length bathroom mirror and then said I was aiming too high. Instead, he said, I should aim for girls who were not as pretty and who were on a "lower level."

Milo's words infuriated me. Who was he? I thought. Who was he to judge who would and would not be a good partner for me? Milo's remark struck a nerve and has reminded me time and time again of two things. One, you must value people for who they are—once you get to know them; and two, never settle. I'm not suggesting that I'm only looking to marry someone model-beautiful with the generosity of Mother Teresa, but I am saying that I'm not going to avoid girls I like just because they're pretty or kind. That makes no sense. Instead, I will always strive for the best I can be and always do the best I can do. Milo may never know that he said something that affected me so profoundly, but he did. At least that's what I heard loud and clear and I will always remember him for that.

■ ■ ■

DURING OUR FRESHMAN year, Duane and I went home to Seymour every weekend. Duane was dating my neighbor, Angie Champ, who along with Toby was a sophomore in high school. It was a nice transition for me to be home so often. That way I could hang out with Toby and our other friends who were between us in age.

About the only thing I was really excited about during my freshman year scholastically was the business fraternity I joined, Delta Sigma Pi. We had an office in the business school and were mostly involved in talking about business, and helping out and hosting philanthropic events. I was not a frat geek, and none of my friends were into fraternities. If they had been, I might have joined one. Then again, maybe not.

The whole commitment thing with a fraternity scared me. In a traditional fraternity, one that had an actual frat house, I was concerned about the layout of the house. Would they have a bathroom that was accessible for me? Could I navigate the house? If my friends were not accepted and I was, who would help me dress and bathe?

Students who were not part of the Greek system called themselves, in jest, GDIs (God—— Independents). Shows you where I was with my faith. Now I would say Gosh Darn Independent, but at the time, while it seemed odd, it was easier to say.

Despite my earlier misgivings about navigating the campus, I really did well and had no more trouble than any other freshman in finding my way—except when the weather was brutally cold and snowy. Muncie, Indiana, happens to be in a windy snow corridor and that created an issue about the safety of my traveling to class on my scooter. My scooter can go just about anywhere, but as with any wheeled vehicle, it is far more dangerous to drive it through snow and ice than it is on pavement or grass.

My freshman year we had two days in a row with below-zero temperatures and a wind chill of sixty-six degrees below zero. Snow was also coming down everywhere. University president John Worthen did not cancel classes, even though a lot of people thought he should have. Instead, he said something to the effect of, "If people can ski in this weather, then they can go to school in this weather." I'm not sure how much President Worthen knew about skiing, because there were no hills in Muncie nearly tall enough to ski down. And I never once saw anyone using cross-country skis.

Rich Harris was of the mind-set that it was too dangerous for me to try to get to class, so someone from his office called and asked me to stay put in my dorm. They were afraid my scooter would freeze up. Like most kids, I was happy to legally skip a few classes! The best part about those two days was that a bunch of girls got "stranded" in our part of the quad and ended up spending the night with us.

During my freshman year, in addition to Milo, Duane was also being paid by a program instituted by the state of Indiana to assist me. How that worked was that I had to fill out paperwork every week, which Duane and Milo then sent to the state so they could get paid.

One day Duane's mom called my mom and informed her quite abruptly that I had not filled out the paperwork for Duane to get paid in some time. This was unacceptable to them. I immediately knew that was not the case and confronted Duane about it. He cleaned off his desk that was piled a mile high with unorganized stacks of papers and found six weeks' worth of forms that I had completed and given to him. Duane was not the neatest, most organized, or most responsible person around.

Later, I was looking for the remote and found a letter Duane had written to Angie, my friend and neighbor and his girlfriend, telling her in detail how much he hated living with me. I had such a devastating feeling when I read that letter. My stomach churned so much I wanted to throw up. Then I got really pissed off. I never get down about life regarding my physical stature, but I occasionally get mad about individual circumstances that it causes.

As with the incident on the phone when Duane laughed to his mother about the idea of my going out with a girl, I never told Duane I had unexpectedly found this letter. I wish now that we both had been mature enough to talk it through. But we weren't. We were just kids. If we had, I think it would have made life easier for both of us. These two deep betrayals from Duane created a mistrust in me with regard to him and, unfortunately, others. It also was just one of many deep layers to our friendship, layers that I didn't even realize were there until many years later.

Duane had his own angst and his own troubles, but that is his story to tell. I can say that Duane is not a bad person. We remain friends, and Duane now has a master's in psychology and works with pedophiles in the prison system. He has a tough job and he does it well. But as you'll see, I wasn't the only trouble he had.

Looking back, I was still so dependent on others for my basic needs when I was in college that I feel it robbed me of many life experiences. On the other hand, it forced me to become closer to my roommates, like Duane, but that closeness in return created depths to our relationship that most friendships do not have. Many times I was temporarily on the outs with a person who was dressing me, bathing me, and helping me to the bathroom, and that forced both of us to reach into ourselves to make it all work. That is not necessarily a bad thing, and I so appreciate my friends' stepping in because it produced a much more "normal" life experience for me than working with an aide did. But frustrations were sometimes high and we all lashed out at whomever we were closest to.

■ ■ ■

FOR OUR SOPHOMORE year, two friends from Seymour, Mike Sutton and Chad Huddleston, joined Duane and me, and the four of us went out on our own and rented a three-bedroom apartment in the Windsong complex, which was adjacent to campus. Duane and I shared one room, and Mike and Chad each had their own room.

I had met Chad in kindergarten, and while we were not best buddies, we were in each other's peripheral circles all the way through graduation. In seventh grade, when a number of elementary schools came together, Chad met Mike and they became friends. Both were jocks, which Duane and I were not, but we all got along well.

Without any guidance or restrictions whatsoever, Duane and Chad began to flounder. I can't tell you the number of battles the four of us had or the number of parties that were held in our front room while I was trying to study in my bedroom in the back. I can't say I was completely innocent in all of this, because I did join in on a lot of the fun, but I balanced it with my studies. Duane and Chad did not and ended up flunking out. Later they were put on probation and Duane went on to graduate.

This apartment complex had a "no pets" rule, but a few months after we moved in they began allowing them. We all decided to get a dog and ended up with a shepherd-chow mix that we named Forest. While Forest was technically Mike Sutton's dog, I lived with her through a series of roommates through my senior year.

Forest was great company, and her presence helped settle tensions that sometimes arose among the four of us. After we all graduated, a friend's sister took her and Forest lived to a ripe old age. She was a big part of my college experience and I consider her a fifth roommate.

I really began to get involved with the Entrepreneurship Program during my sophomore year. Not many sophomores were interested in the entrepreneurship club, but I was and I felt so elated and worthy to be involved.

■ ■ ■

LIKE MOST COLLEGE kids, I wanted a job, because a job meant money and money meant freedom. I researched my options and decided to apply at Wal-Mart. I was hired the summer after my sophomore year as a people greeter. It was, and still is, the only job I have ever had where I have had to clock in and out.

I loved the job, though. What a fantastic opportunity to meet people! It also gave me the chance to see firsthand how a larger business operates. I don't know about now, but back then at this particular store, to use an old metaphor regarding their management structure, there were too many chiefs and not enough Indians.

As an example, during training, I was taught never to point a finger to tell a customer where something was. We were to show them. Well, I got in trouble with one manager for leaving my post to show a customer the location of whatever it was that she needed. After that I was moved to the garden center, which was a lot more laid-back.

During my two summers at Wal-Mart, I worked mostly with older, semiretired people. This was great because these coworkers typically had the flexibility to swap schedules, which was awesome for a socially active teenager like me.

I developed a lot of friendships at Wal-Mart, including one with a man named Buck. Buck was a short, wiry guy in his eighties who had a never-ending supply of dirty jokes and who incessantly complained that it had been thirteen years since his wife of more than fifty years had slept with him.

My heavyset friend Bubba (who was involved in the infamous malt-tossing incident) worked in the sporting goods department, and it wasn't long before I knew just about everyone who worked in the store. I learned a lot there, but when the next summer rolled around I thought it would be cool to work somewhere else and see how that business ran.

I applied at a local national footwear brand outlet store for several reasons. One, they had better hours than those I was working at Wal-Mart, and two, a few really cute girls worked there that I wanted to get to know better.

A friend worked at the store and told me about the job opening. But when I applied in person, the manager told me they were not hiring. I called my friend back and she said, "That's not true. They *are* hiring." I called the manager and told him I knew they were hiring and asked him why he had told me they were not. He said it was because, due to my size, there was nothing I could do at the store. Excuse me. Have you ever heard of a cash register? I could have worked the register.

It is beyond frustrating to me when someone tells me I can't do something without giving me the opportunity to try. Despite my physical limitations, I am a capable, reliable, dependable person who can do a lot more than you might think. I have a great attitude and excel in working with people.

This manager's comments really pissed me off and I got livid.

How dare he? In thinking it through, I realized that if he had acted this way toward me, which by the way is illegal, he was doing it to others, too. I decided to sue not for my own gain, but to let this man know that his actions were improper and to stop it from happening in the future.

To help me, I got the EEOC involved. The Equal Employment Opportunity Commission is a government agency that enforces federal laws against discrimination on the base of race, color, religion, sex, national origin, age, or disability. We ended up settling out of court for a sum that was about equal to what I would have been paid had I worked at the national footwear brand store for the summer.

The end result was that I stayed at Wal-Mart for another summer, which was fine. There was still a lot to learn from that operation.

■　■　■

OUR JUNIOR YEAR we all moved to a five-bedroom house on North Ball Avenue. Mike Sutton's friend John Bachert had pretty much lived with us in the apartment our sophomore year and moved with us to the house. With my roommates and their girlfriends, there were usually about nine people living there.

The house had originally been a two-bedroom, but our landlord had built three additional bedrooms onto the back of the structure. Those rooms were tiny, with the actual beds up in lofts. Because getting up into a loft bed every night would have been very difficult, I ended up with one of the original, and bigger, bedrooms at the front of the house.

This was both a blessing and a curse, because while my room was big enough to fit my bed and my scooter, it was also closer to the kitchen, and no one in that house cleaned. I mean no one. The smell from the kitchen sometimes got so bad that I gagged when I opened my bedroom door. When we moved out of that house the amount of stuff that was thrown away was amazing: toaster ovens and microwaves that were way beyond use, and bags and bags and bags of trash. It was disgusting.

That said, there were a lot of other houses near campus that were in worse shape than ours. One house had a keg party every Thursday night and charged three dollars for a cup. That's how those kids paid their rent, with proceeds from the parties.

One weekend Toby and a few of our friends were up from Seymour and we were all at a house party when it got busted. The police took the beer tap and told all of us to leave. In taking the tap, there was no way to get the beer out of the keg. Some kids were smart enough to have a second tap, but that was not the case in this instance. Besides, the police were firm in saying we didn't have to go home, but we couldn't stay there. We got out pretty fast! That was one of several close calls that we had in college, but I never was arrested, probably because I never drove to any of the parties. Instead, I was always sure to take my scooter, and my roommates walked.

I have to say that we had our own share of parties at our house. That was another disadvantage of the location of my bedroom. It was much closer to the living room than the bedrooms in the back. If I didn't want to party, the noise was pretty brutal.

I definitely did my share of partying in college (when I was a sophomore my roommates and I went through a half gallon of Jim Beam a night and that hadn't changed much by the time I was a senior). It was my upbringing as a kid not to go to a party unless I was specifically invited. In college, that's not how it worked. Most parties were free-for-alls and I always felt a little strange just showing up, even if I was with my friends. It worked the other way, too. If we were having a party, you never knew who, or how many, would walk through the door. Of course, the more people, the more girls. Also, the bigger the mess.

All of my roommates and their friends smoked Marlboro Lights. Back then they had "Marlboro Miles" on each package. These were like coupons or points. As I was the first one up every morning, despite the overwhelming smell of smoke, I went around the house and collected all the Marlboro Miles and cashed them in through a catalog system. I got a lot of cool stuff, including a Swiss Army knife and a tent. Because I didn't smoke, those rewards helped me put up with the constant smell.

One day a couple of us had had enough. We called a house meeting and asked the girlfriends (who pretty much lived there but were not paying rent) if they could at least chip in for toilet paper and other household items. We also all agreed that we could do a better job of picking up, washing dishes, and taking out the trash. Of course, I did what I could, but I was limited physically. It got better for a while.

Eventually, however, it turned into a "pick your battle" situation and more than one of us realized that including the girlfriends in the responsibility of keeping the house clean and well-stocked was one of those battles we could not continually win. It was a great lesson, though. As I headed into my senior year, and in the years to come, I would have lot of battles ahead of me in life—and a couple of wars—including but not limited to a bankruptcy, the loss of my mother, and several relationships that I was hopeful about but never went anywhere.

COMMITMENT: THE TRUE
MEANING FOR ME

Since I was in middle school I had been dreaming of owning a restaurant. I know that some of you reading this book have had your own romantic fantasy of being served in your own eatery! In pursuit of my dream I had been collecting menus for years. Pizza menus, steak house menus, breakfast menus, you name it, I had a stack of them.

I think I developed a real appreciation for restaurants because when I was young it was always a special event when we went out. Mom was such a great cook that we rarely went to a restaurant, but when we did, it was always somewhere nice. These special occasions fueled my fire to have a restaurant of my own.

A lot of the menus came from our trips to Wisconsin. There, along with Grandma and Grandpa Wilson, we'd eat the fish we caught one night, and the next night we'd all go out to eat, usually at one of the local supper clubs. These restaurants all had diverse menus, from steak to salads to seafood, and somehow a copy of every menu made its way onto my scooter.

One restaurant in particular, the Pub N' Prime, had the best prime rib I'd ever eaten—I mean the very best. The owner was a single mom with two boys and she often took time to talk with us. It was through these conversations that I gained a real appreciation of the nuances of restaurant ownership and all it entailed.

The Whitetail Inn was another place we often went to. It was housed in a giant log cabin and I got it in my mind that I, too, would have a log cabin structure for my restaurant. I took away from that business a lot of details about design and structure, and stored all of it in my mind for future reference.

In the middle of my junior year of college, I began thinking more about how I could make my restaurant a reality. I knew I wanted to build my restaurant from scratch, so I began sketching floor plans and fine-tuning menus. Even though no one ever explicitly said to me, "Fred, you can do this," it never occurred to me that I couldn't or wouldn't. There was no question in my mind that I would always work for myself and that I'd have my own restaurant someday. I just didn't have all the pieces of the puzzle worked out yet.

Much later someone commented, "If you want to be in the restaurant industry just take ten thousand dollars, go to the most expensive restaurant you can find in New York City, spend five thousand for the meal and the tip, then flush the other five grand down the toilet. Then you can say you've been in the restaurant business and only lost ten thousand dollars."

I wish I could say that.

Another joke in regard to working for yourself is that you

only work half a day; you even get to pick which twelve hours you work.

If I'd heard those things before I started my restaurant, I might have listened. But probably not. This was my dream and I was so close to making it happen I could taste it. Looking back, I don't think anything could have deterred me.

My goal was to have a restaurant up and running as soon as I graduated. You might think this was ambitious, if even possible, because I had never even worked at a restaurant. That is true, but I had been studying them as long as I could remember. But before I could open the doors to my dream, I had to finish my senior year—and graduate.

■ ■ ■

FOR MY FINAL year at Ball State, Chad and I moved into a house on Neely Avenue six houses down from campus. This house had a basement—a really wet basement—that had a bedroom that our third roommate, Jeremy Jaynes, lived in. Jeremy was a younger friend from Seymour.

I don't see how Jeremy did it. At times, it was so damp down there that his socks were continually wet. And the smell. It couldn't have been healthy. Chad got a Rottweiler puppy and in our spare time we'd all sit on the porch with a cold beer and watch the girls go by as they headed to class. Except for the wet basement, it was an awesome house.

The other interesting thing about this year was that Toby was on campus as a freshman, as was Josh, Chad's brother. Josh was a great kid who recently lost a battle with leukemia. It was a blow to all of us who knew and loved him. I look forward to talking baseball with Josh again someday.

Unlike me, and extremely unlike Toby, my brother took his chances with the roommate lottery and it could not have worked out better. Kurt Anderson to this day is still Toby's best friend. Plus, although Kurt has three brothers of his own, he is like a second brother to me. As Toby was a freshman studying human resources, I didn't see him all that often, but it was great having him close. Mostly I saw him when he came to our house for a party or when he wanted one of my roommates or me to buy alcohol—although he rarely drank. We always obliged.

The capstone course requirement for Dr. K was that his students develop an extensive business plan. I didn't have to present it until the spring but I wanted to get a jump start on it. Without a doubt, this was the most important thing I had done in my life so far, so I was very methodical. I didn't want to leave anything out or have the smallest contingency unaccounted for. I haven't always had that attention to detail, but I am glad I did then.

I started in our college of business's resource center, as it had all of the plans from previous students, and I wanted to learn what they did right and wrong. Only the successful plans were archived here. I often checked out the plans so I could take them home, then cross-referenced them so I could have detailed information at my fingertips.

This attention to detail would also prove useful in the future. When my best friend, John Rich, appeared on *The Celebrity Apprentice*, I prepared for him a two-inch-thick binder of all the previous contestants, detailing their strengths and weaknesses and where they ended up in the competition. John won and later told me how much the binder helped. I had learned well during my many years as a Boy Scout. Always be prepared.

Because I ate, lived, and breathed my business plan during my senior year, I inadvertently neglected some of my other duties. This included the meeting attendance policy at my business fraternity. That neglect almost got me kicked out, but the other members realized that my major was a demanding one. Plus, they realized that freshmen don't always know what kind of a workload they will carry as a senior and can't be held to commitments they made almost four years earlier. When everyone voted about whether or not I would be able to remain as a member, I was very pleased that I got to stay. It's a good fraternity that helps worthy causes. However, there are only twenty-four hours in a day and I was busy twenty-five of them.

That fall I finished up classes and excelled in business management, international business, and marketing. I also had the opportunity to take a few days off from classes and go with Dad to the National Restaurant Association's trade show in Chicago. The event was held at McCormick Place, one of the country's premier and largest convention facilities, and I have to say that I was more than a little awed.

It seemed as if there were a thousand exhibitors, and Dad and I stopped to talk with everyone. Some of them blew us off, but others took a sincere interest in me—and in my desire to own a restaurant. This was the first thing Dad and I had done together regarding the restaurant business and I was like a kid in a candy store. I loved being with Dad, and I loved learning more about the business of restaurant ownership. We were there for three days and came away with a new understanding of all that was involved in making my dream become a reality.

Dad really took one for the team by giving me his full attention and by indulging me in stopping by all the booths and carrying all the materials I picked up. This is especially admirable because before I became involved he was not all that interested in the restaurant business. I want to thank my dad for that time in Chicago.

A few weeks after the conference, something unexpected happened. A dive bar called Mill Street Tavern on Third and Mill Street in Seymour came up for sale, lock, stock, and barrel. A local Realtor knew of my passion for the restaurant business and alerted me that the business was for sale. It had been owned by three couples that were once all great friends. Unfortunately, neither the friendships nor the restaurant survived.

Despite my dream to build a log-cabin-style restaurant from the ground up, this was an opportunity I could not pass by. But I was a student with no funds. How could I make this happen? First I wrote a small version of what would eventually become my full business plan. Then I did some out-of-the-box thinking and over the course of about six weeks, with the help of my parents and a creative banker, I was able to structure the needed financing. By the time I returned to school from Christmas break, the deal was in place. Where there is a will there is a way, and I kept asking until the no turned into a yes.

■ ■ ■

MY LAST SEMESTER of college I arranged it so I only had classes on Tuesdays and Thursdays. This meant I could spend

Friday through Monday, as needed, in Seymour gathering data and doing research. I approached this task like a full-time job. I knew I wanted to call the restaurant Fred N' Toby's Restaurant and Bar, because everyone in Seymour and the surrounding area knew us as Fred and Toby, due to our stature. One thing I'd learned along the way was the importance of name recognition and branding, and I wanted to capitalize on that.

There was also an assumption on my part that Toby would join me full-time after he graduated. He, in fact, did, but I do not think that was his first choice. I wish now that I had been more conscious of what he wanted to do in life, versus what I wanted for him. He had a degree in human resources, so running a restaurant probably did not play to his strengths. But back then, in my mind, it was all about me.

Much of my research took the form of surveys and when the dust settled I had developed and facilitated one hundred twenty of them. I polled the residents of Seymour and the surrounding areas on everything from menu items and price points to things like atmosphere and hours of operation. In addition to research being another class requirement, I was getting some great information that helped me finalize my business plan.

I was also busy with permits, zoning, codes, remodeling, costs, and striking early deals with vendors. It was one of the busiest times of my life and I loved every second of it. I really felt like I could run a restaurant better than the next guy and was thrilled that I had a chance to prove myself right. Of course, I did not want to stop with one restaurant. I already had dreams of franchising.

But first I wanted to spend some time during spring break

with Toby and some of our friends in Panama City Beach, Florida. There were about twelve of us all packed into one room, and just two beds, but because I drove I got one of the beds and because Toby was my brother, he shared the bed with me.

As I've mentioned, I was starved for female intimacy. While other guys my age were getting it on with their girlfriends, I was still giving neck massages. I was desperate for more. I found out that there was one strip bar in the area and I was bound and determined I was going to go. I'd never been before and I was curious. I was also so over-the-top hormonal that I couldn't stand it.

I talked some of my friends who were on the trip into going with me. Toby was not one of them. Some of the guys had been to a strip club before and told me what to expect. That night I spent about sixty dollars in one-dollar bills at the edge of the stage. I had the best time. Unfortunately, this initial experience quickly turned into an obsession that impaired my focus on business and landed me in a lot of debt.

■ ■ ■

TWO WEEKS BEFORE graduation, I turned my business plan in to Dr. Kuratko. I wish I could express how grateful I am for the chance to study under this man. It was a true privilege to learn from someone who pushed all his students to excel far beyond what we ever thought we could. Almost fifteen years out of college I still think of him nearly every day. He made that much of an impact on me.

I wish everyone had a role model, a mentor, like Dr. Kuratko. If they did, I believe there would be a lot more people who are passionate about their chosen profession. Dr. Kuratko was a given when I was accepted at Ball State, but if you don't have a mentor like him in your life, find someone. There are a lot of good people who are willing and able to nurture someone along—if you have a burning desire to succeed and are willing to put the time in to do so.

Dr. K had a board of more than sixty businessmen and -women. These entrepreneurship experts and past entrepreneurship graduates were divided into panels of six who reviewed each student's business plan a week before the student's presentation of it. I would have to be grilled successfully by one of these panels if I were to pass and graduate.

Dr. K's father told him that if his students' spines did not sweat when they were in bed thinking about their business plan then the course was not tough enough. Overall, it was a true spine-sweating experience.

On Monday the week I was to graduate, my classmates and I caravanned to Indianapolis together. We went to Indianapolis because a vice president at Blue Cross Blue Shield, Mike Houlk, was on our board and donated the use of Blue Cross's prestigious conference rooms for our reviews. Plus, it was a central location for the reviewers, who were all professionals and their time was money. We each had half an hour to present our plan and another half hour to answer questions from this board of experts. We had been told (and we understood very clearly) that there would be no excuses allowed if we didn't show up on time for our individual presentations, so we traveled together, just in case one of us had car trouble. It was that important.

If our individual panel from Dr. K's board thought a plan was viable, the student would receive an A and graduate on time. If they didn't, the student would fail and not graduate with the entrepreneurship degree. It was a true pass/fail situation and I learned before I went in that in more than twenty years, Dr. K had never overturned a failing grade that was given by the board.

A few students had a safety net of a dual major in business management. Most of us, however, myself included, had staked our entire college education—and for me, the money my parents had spent on it—on this single day.

Some of the areas I was grilled on included intricate knowledge of three years' worth of forecasted financials (done on an Excel spreadsheet, rather than in a program such as Quicken or QuickBooks). This included income statements, balance sheets, cash flow, and a break-even analysis all created from the ground up, and it all had to balance. I spent hundreds of hours building the financials and it taught me a lot about Excel. It gave me such a love for number crunching that I now have the symbol for pi tattooed in red on my left shoulder. I was also grilled on logistics, the completeness of the plan, and my knowledge of the restaurant business in general.

I was in a class of just sixteen and going in I was very confident. After all, I had lived this plan for the last several years. I had studied, prepared, and researched, and you know what? It paid off. I knew my stuff. As an ace in the hole, I had my approved bank financing documentation in my briefcase, but I did not have to pull that out one time.

In the end, four people failed, one did not even present, and eleven people passed. I was one of those eleven. I also received the highest honor from the panel that could be given, the Entrepreneur in Excellence Award.

I graduated May 10, 1997, and was thrilled to attend my graduation ceremony for Ball State's College of Business. In addition to Dr. K, Dr. Jeff Hornsby also had a large impact as a mentor. Dr. Hornsby was also the director of the human resources program Toby graduated from. He is now at Kansas State as the director of the Entrepreneurship Program there.

Maggie Ailes was Dr. K's right arm and I don't know what we all would have done without her help and input. I credit these three people, plus many of my other professors and College of Business dean Neil Palomba, with my educational accomplishments.

I skipped the main Ball State graduation ceremony. The bar was set so high after making it through the Entrepreneurship Program that I didn't want to be let down by another graduation event. Plus, I was so gung-ho about getting the restaurant going that I didn't have time. I moved home to my parents' house right after graduation and took ownership of the building on May 22.

My biggest regret for several years after I graduated was that I did not take the year after college off to travel, relax, and ponder what life had in store. I was so focused on the restaurant that I didn't, and couldn't, consider anything else. In my typical fashion I chose to jump at the chance to purchase an existing restaurant and building that had a long history in my hometown. At that point my thought was "What could be better than that?" Ummm . . .

In hindsight, if I hadn't done things that I later regretted doing, I wouldn't be where I am now. Since then I have realized that God has a plan, and the very thing I regretted miss-ing is exactly what He has given me many times over, which is freedom and unbelievable travels. As an entertainer, I have made many trips crisscrossing the country and abroad. I have learned a lot from my travels, but not nearly as much as I did in opening and operating the restaurant. We were set to open in just eight weeks and one of the wildest rides of my life was about to start. I couldn't wait!

SWEET DREAMS ARE NOT ALWAYS AS SWEET AS THEY SEEM

The moment I held the keys to the restaurant in my hand was one of the sweetest moments of my life. All my entrepreneurial efforts, experience, and dreams, and all my planning, had only partially prepared me for the huge swell of pride that coursed through my veins. *I* had a restaurant! I *had* a restaurant! I had a *restaurant*!

There was a lot to do before the much-anticipated opening day, but first things first. We had to celebrate my college graduation. Even though remodeling began right away, the bar was already stocked with inventory from the previous business. To prepare for my party, my dad and I went to the restaurant to get mixers and cans of V8. As we loaded them into my van, I mentioned that we should write down what we took so we could balance inventory.

"Are you kidding?" Dad asked. "I made it possible for you to pay for this stuff and you seriously want to charge me?"

He was really perturbed. That was the first inkling I had that my parents did not have a clue about retail business, or more specifically, the restaurant business. Even though Mom and Dad had run their service-based businesses very well for so many years, Dad didn't understand anything about inventory. I just wanted to have accurate records for accounting purposes. It was a dawning moment of realization that changed my perception and judgment on many things. I saw a side of my dad that day that I did not realize existed. Much later in life I realized a boundary had been broken that day and it took a lot of time and effort to repair it.

In business you have to have guidelines. That moment created a looseness in my mind about the way we did business that snowballed into buying, budgeting, and profit and loss. Unfortunately, this was not the last argument we'd have about the business end of the restaurant.

The next weeks were slammed with an abundant amount of remodeling and construction. The building had been a restaurant or dive bar since the 1940s and had evolved many times, so there was a lot to do to turn it into the classy vision I had for Fred N' Toby's. One thing we were not going to change was the back bar itself. The bar was unique in that it had originally come from the 1893 Chicago World's Fair. It was a long, ornate cherrywood bar that was hand carved by the Brunswick Corporation, our country's oldest manufacturer of bar fixtures. I later spent many nights sitting at that bar drinking way too much with friends and regular customers.

We opened on July 26, 1997, the day before my twenty-third birthday, and even before we opened we had problems. I had kept a lot of the staff that the previous owners had employed, including a husband-and-wife management team, and they had their own ideas about how things should go. These ideas, of course, were in direct contrast to mine. In hindsight, I was pretty headstrong about my ideas and probably was not very diplomatic in how I implemented them. But on the other hand, a lot of it was a small-town mentality and my staff did not want to adapt to change of any sort. From a more recent point of view, I am glad they wanted to take some sense of ownership about their jobs, but we butted heads a lot, which added to the already mounting stress of opening day.

The next step was to hire a chef, and I was so pleased to find one with great references right out of culinary school. He and I worked hard on finalizing the menu and setting up the kitchen. Toby pitched in by picking up much-needed and last-minute pieces of equipment. It was a lot of long, hard hours for all of us.

I was thrilled when all of our work paid off with a very successful "friends and family" soft opening the night before the big day. While we all thought we were ready for the official opening I don't think any of us were prepared for the huge volume of customers that came to Seymour's newest restaurant. It was great! In fact, it was fantastic. The house was packed and everyone's expectations were not only met, they were exceeded. Our rookie chef was overwhelmed, but he dug in to handle the fast pace and stress that came along with it. However, he was about to be married and his fiancée did not support the commitment he had to Fred N' Toby's. Long story short, he didn't return after opening night.

Talk about jumping from the frying pan into the fire. Here I was, on the second day, and I didn't have a chef. I was so lucky that with a lot of scrambling my other staff picked up the slack, and I found a new executive chef within days.

With my new chef, though, I learned that sometimes you have to be careful what you wish for. First of all, he claimed he had once worked as a chef at the White House. Yes, *the* White House, the one where the president lives. I don't know how I could have been so gullible. But he made amazing pies and it seemed like he could handle the kitchen without too much trouble.

It wasn't too long, however, before things about him started not to add up. I have a file-cabinet-like memory and cross-reference things in my mind intuitively. One day I was going through invoices and found receipts for chocolate pies. The wonderful pies he convinced me he made from scratch he was buying from our main supplier! Turned out I caught him in a lot of other things he told me that were not true, and I fired this pathological liar before more damage was done.

You can imagine the morale my staff had in losing two chefs in a short period of time. It was about as low as it could go. On top of that, we were still ironing out details that arose from opening a new business. This included staff turnover, computer systems, inventory control, and the cash register.

We had purchased a then-state-of-the-art point-of-sale touch-screen register system because it was harder for employees to steal cash from this system than conventional registers. While it worked great, we figured out by day two that we needed a second terminal. Having just the one station for our waitstaff slowed down the transaction process so much that it made customers wait longer than they needed—and most of all, as the owner, more than I wanted them to.

■ ■ ■

THAT FIRST YEAR and a half was rough from the second we opened, and a lot of my stress was due to the fact that I kept having to go to my parents for cash for things like payroll and a second POS terminal. Back then a terminal ran about five thousand dollars. All of the money for these unexpected expenses came from my dad's 401(k), which I have since found out is a big no-no. If you ever have thoughts about dipping into your parents' 401(k) for something you think you need, learn from me and don't. If you are unable to pay it back, as I was, it will not be soon forgotten.

Even before I fired the second chef, the business side of the restaurant was spiraling. We needed an influx of stability and that came in the form of a man named Mike Bostock. Mikey, as we called him, was a Vietnam vet who happened to be one of the best cooks around. He lived in a trailer in a neighboring town about ten miles from Fred N' Toby's and hitchhiked to and from work. Food-wise, he held the restaurant together for a long time. It was a great relief to have a chef I could count on. I really liked Mikey and was taken aback and saddened when I learned of his passing some years later.

Another pillar of stability came in the form of Inge Boughman. I inherited Inge from the previous owners and I think they inherited her from the owners before that. Inge was a divorced German mom in her sixties who served as our dishwasher. While I always knew our dishes would be spotless, Inge had a temper. Inge liked me as a boss, but part of my job turned into being a peacekeeper between her and the rest of the kitchen staff.

After spending so many years in the building Inge also claimed there was a ghost in the dish room that could be her father. We jokingly named the "ghost" Gus, but I have to say, the dish room was creepy in the dark. Who is to say Inge wasn't right? Ghosts aside, Inge was always the first one in, every day. In addition to dishes, she cleaned the bathrooms and the entire restaurant. We had the cleanest place in town, and it was all due to Inge's diligence and impeccable work.

Despite the steadiness that staff such as Inge, Mikey, and others brought to Fred N' Toby's, I was finding that the restaurant business was a lot of work. Not that I minded, but I hadn't counted on the amount of stress that was involved due to staffing inadequacies. Adding to the stress was the fact that Mom and Dad were supportive of the restaurant, but I got the feeling they thought I should be there 24/7. Rather than being able to talk through problems with them, as I wish I could have, they made comments that implied, "This is your deal, you'd better make it work." So I did—as best I could. In the process I often sacrificed a lot more than I should have.

■ ■ ■

ABOUT A YEAR after we opened Fred N' Toby's, a customer told me about a spa in Louisville where you could get a massage and whatever else you wanted for under a hundred bucks. Within a few days, I was on my way there. I was nervous as heck, but the lack of female interaction and the lack of female touch made me crave it all the more.

When I arrived, I parked my van in the back parking lot, just as my friend had told me to. I used my sticks to walk to the door and knocked instead of using the buzzer, as the buzzer was too high for me to reach. A tiny, elderly oriental woman let me in and in broken English said, "Wait just minute."

A pretty girl retrieved me from the plush waiting area and held a finger up to her mouth, asking me to be quiet. I followed her to a room where two more oriental women helped me onto a table. They washed me, inspected my private parts, helped me down, gave me a towel, and led me to a plush massage room. Here, a beautiful oriental girl with large breasts gave me a wonderful massage.

After, she asked, "You cop?" When I told her I wasn't she asked if I wanted more. Yes, I did! By this time I was pretty excited. It was the first ejaculation I ever had other than with myself.

When I left I was glowing. The experience was kind and gentle, and even though I had paid for it, I won't lie: I look back on it fondly. Over the years I found that because I was not a physical threat to these girls, they could relax with me. Maybe because of that I got a better quality of service than someone else might have had. At least I'd like to think so.

I went back three or four times over the next six or eight months. The spa was not too far from a gambling boat I frequented in New Albany, Indiana, so I could gamble after I'd seen the girls. I hope it's obvious, but I still have to add that I do not condone illegal sex services. I understand that not everyone is in it by choice, but I was. And, as you'll read, not all of my experiences were positive.

■ ■ ■

IN AN UNCONSCIOUS effort to make things right at the restaurant, rather than scale back I decided we needed another income source, so I built Gilly's. Gilly's was a pizza delivery and take-out place at the back of the restaurant. That turned out to be one of the better moves I ever made, and a big part of Gilly's initial success was due to Terry Whipple. Terry had worked at every pizza place in town and knew the business inside and out. I had originally hired Terry as a cook at Fred N' Toby's but with his pizza experience it was a no-brainer for him to run Gilly's.

With the help of suppliers, we developed our own dough, sauce, and recipes. I didn't allow pizza to be sold in Fred N' Toby's. People had to purchase it from Gilly's. Since then I have questioned that decision, but Fred N' Toby's was a classy steak house. Besides, it could not handle the volume of both sets of customers.

Initially it was a nice problem to have, owning a restaurant that was too busy. But at thirty-five hundred square feet, and with a tiny food-prep area, we could not handle the crowd and from day one we had issues with flow from the kitchen. If I had to do it over again (which thank God I don't), I would increase prices and that would cut back naturally on volume.

Dad was always in my head about prices. He thought they should be kept as low as possible. I had learned that if you looked at issues of affordable prices, quality meals, and top service as points on a triangle, the rule of thumb is that to be successful you can only have two out of the three. My mistake was that we tried to be all three. For example, to have top-quality food and excellent service, you have to charge high prices, and we didn't do that.

Another factor was my physical inability to jump in and do what was needed to fill any void. That was extremely frustrating, and oftentimes maddening. My lifelong dream was turning into a nightmarish situation. It was spiraling out of control and that created more stress than I could handle. One night Mom and Dad came in for dinner, which they did quite often, and had a terrible experience. Mom tried to get Dad to leave but he felt it was necessary to stop by the office and express his negative opinion. It was the last thing I needed, especially that night as I was so beaten down.

I thought back to when I was younger and had such an appreciation and gratitude for the simple things in life. Somewhere recently I had lost that. I lost it in the rejection of women and the stresses of owning the restaurant of my dreams. I lost it in the everyday disappointments of life and in the delicate balance of maintaining a happy staff and maintaining a successful business.

That night there was so much stress and I had so much anxiety that I crawled under my desk and lay hidden from the world in a fetal position. I had pushed so hard to get Fred N' Toby's off the ground and running. Now I didn't know what to do. I wish I had been in a place where I could have called out to God for help, but I wasn't there yet. I know now that He was watching over me, that this situation taught me things I needed to know, that it shaped me into who I am today. That night, however, I didn't know any of that. I just know that I woke up the next morning in a cold sweat with the understanding that I had to do something. So I buckled down and did it.

It was trial by fire. I increased advertising and began stopping by WJAA, a local radio station, to promote Fred N' Toby's even more. A former Global Wrestling Federation wrestler from Seymour, Rip Rogers, often stopped by the station as well. He was also head trainer at the facility of Ohio Valley Wrestling, which was a developmental league for WWE.

Somehow we came up with the idea to stage a tag-team wrestling tournament during the station's annual Bus Stock festival. It would be the station's lunchtime jock, Rick Wilson (the Meatpacker), and Toby (Little Sexy) against Doctor Dave, a local pawnshop owner and advertiser with the station, and me (the Red Hornet).

We actually had two matches. One was at the festival and the other was at the restaurant. My team won the first match and Toby's the second. If you weren't one of the hundred or so people who were there, a video of it exists and will probably show up on YouTube at some point. Be sure to subscribe to my YouTube channel at www.youtube.com/TwoFootFred.

Wrestling was fun, but I had more fixing to do. I opened two more Gilly's locations, one in Columbus, Indiana, and one in Crothersville, Indiana. Each town is about twenty miles from Seymour, so the locations were far enough apart to attract a wide base of customers, yet close enough that I could be at any location quickly.

The Columbus location had been a pizza place before we took over, and we learned the hard way that the place was jinxed. We did better than anyone else in that location but ended up shutting it down seven or eight months after we opened. Some buildings just do not do well as retail operations and this was one of those places.

The Gilly's in Crothersville was in the back of a service station. The town was small, just three thousand people, but Terry, the manager of the Gilly's in Seymour, was from there and thought we would do well. In fact, his aunt Gayle was an experienced pizza maker from Domino's and we "stole" her to run the store. We did well, but not nearly well enough. The town was just too small and there is only so much pizza that people can eat.

While I was still covering the lease on the Columbus location, even though we had closed, Mom and Dad stepped in to cover the lease on the now-closed Crothersville location. I was quickly realizing just how thin I was spread. I needed more hours in the day and more days in the week. I had also gotten to a point where we were experiencing severe cash-flow problems in each of the businesses and I was robbing Peter to pay Paul.

Instead of taking time off to figure out how to make just Fred N' Toby's work, I had mistakenly taken on more and more businesses to, in my mind, satisfy my parents and make things right. And on their end, rather than fix a problem, Mom and Dad were more comfortable putting a Band-Aid on things by injecting the exact amount of cash that would solve the immediate fire of the day. Band-Aids and cash only last so long.

One of the major problems with Fred N' Toby's was theft. It is a big issue in the restaurant business and we always seemed to be short of either cash or supplies. Both affected the bottom line. Plus, I often found certain employees smoking pot in the freezer or cigarettes in the basement. I was so stressed that after initial tantrums to discipline them to get them to quit, I slowly began living the lifestyle of those employees and joined them. And we drank. A lot. Every night. My choice was Crown and Coke.

The stress I was living with caused another major problem in my life. Gambling. Years earlier, during one of our summer vacations to Wisconsin, Toby and I had convinced our parents and grandparents to go to a nearby Indian casino. Toby and I played with five-dollar chips and we each made over one hundred dollars. We were just killing it. Neither of us was of legal age yet, but no one questioned us. The pit bosses and casino staff rooted for us and we all had a great time. Well, everyone except Grandpa Wilson. He was the least enthused and eventually sat in the car to wait for us.

Then, in college, I had grown an affinity for trading stock options, which is a form of legal and accessible gambling. And I had some success. By the time I graduated I had made ten or twelve thousand dollars.

A few events like that planted a seed in the back of my head that gambling was both fun and profitable. In the midst of the troubles with my businesses I decided I needed a break, so Toby and I went to Vegas with a couple buddies. Mom gave Toby and me each a thousand dollars and I went through mine like water. Then I racked up a scary amount of debt on my credit card. While we were there I got totally wasted—several times. Then we visited strip clubs and drank some more. I vomited in public on more than one occasion and even got so drunk that I fell off my scooter and banged my head on the concrete.

This was not the first time I had driven my scooter while under the influence, nor would it be the last. My scooter has armrests that fold up and down. When I was drinking in a bar I often sat on an armrest of my scooter. This way I was eye level with women and they didn't have to look down. Several times after a

was all smiles at age three and a half when Toby was born. Note the corrective shoes I am wearing. I had to wear those shoes twenty-four hours a day, even in bed. My surgery for clubfeet would take place in just a few weeks.

At age four I was unknowingly preparing for the "Save a Horse (Ride a Cowboy)" video at Halloween when I trick-or-treated at Aunt Linda's house.

After my success with my Pinewood Derby car, I was really excited about winning the Cub Scout Space Derby.

I sold my parents on the concept of getting a go-kart when I was ten. It was great to get to spend time with my dad modifying it so I could drive by myself.

Here at age fourteen with my brother Toby (I'm on the right), I started rowing a small boat a little too far from the dock on South Two Lake during one of our Wisconsin vacations. He was glad to get back.

Grandpa Wilson watches while Mom takes my picture during my seventeenth birthday celebration. We were always in Wisconsin on vacation during my birthday.

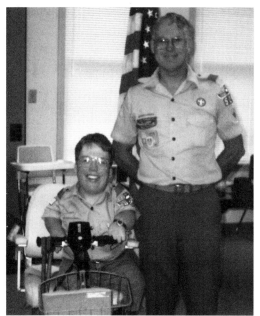

Here I am at age eighteen with Scoutmaster Ron Nelson. Mr. Nelson pushed me to complete all of the requirements for the Eagle Scout award. Thank you, Ron!

"Hi, welcome to Wal-Mart!" I worked as a people greeter in the garden center at Wal-Mart for two summers during college. It was then that I vowed to never work for "the man" again, and I haven't.

The founder and former director of Ball State University's esteemed entrepreneurship program, Dr. Donald F. Kuratko, "Dr. K," and me. Not only had I just passed the spine-sweating experience of presenting my business plan, it was an award-winning presentation.

After Fred N' Toby's became a reality, Gilly's Pizza was my next venture.

Karate expert Superfoot stopped by Fred N' Toby's in 1998.

Singer-songwriter and Seymour native John Cougar Mellencamp and his wife at the time, Elaine Irwin, came by Fred N' Toby's for a meal on Mother's Day in 1998.

Because of my dad's long local political career, Becky Skillman, who was an Indiana state senator at the time, was a family friend. She later became a two-term lieutenant governor of Indiana.

The entire Gill family. *First row, left to right:* Theresa Trimpe Koch, Linda Trimpe, Rick Trimpe, Fred Gill, Toby Gill. *Second row, left to right:* Bob Koch, Casey Regruth, Evan Koch, Carson Regruth, Jennifer Trimpe Regruth. *Third row, left to right:* Grandma Gill, Tyler's girlfriend, Tyler Gill, Brant Handloser, Trey Koch, Braeden Handloser. *Fourth row, left to right:* Uncle Ted Gill, Laura Trimpe Handloser, Drew Handloser, Mark Handloser, J.C. Handloser, Jonathan Gill, Fred's mom, Fred's dad. *Fifth row:* Joh Regruth.

I'm not sure if LeAnn Rimes is smiling at the camera or laughing at my hat. Fan Fair 1999.

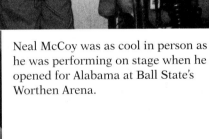

Neal McCoy was as cool in person as he was performing on stage when he opened for Alabama at Ball State's Worthen Arena.

Little did I know during Fan Fair 1999 that five years later I would be out on tour with Tim McGraw. Faith Hill is still tickled over a comment I made during the meet-and-greet.

This was the day after I met John Rich. I love the Warren Brothers poster in the background! That was the year they got in trouble at the Wild Horse Saloon for breaking the new nondrinking-on-stage policy. Love you, Brad and Brett.

Toby's college graduation with Mom and Dad. Toby and I are both Ball State alums. Thank you, Mom and Dad, for taking care of our college education.

The last day of the Tim McGraw tour, Starwood Amphitheatre, Nashville, Tennessee, 2004. Tim had this outfit made for me and during the show he introduced Kenny Chesney. As the crowd went nuts, here I came rolling out. It was a great gag and something right up my alley.

This year we celebrated at Mom and Dad's house. Mom made my favorite chocolate cake. Mom was a great cook and baker.

Here I am shooting a Chevy commercial for the MuzikMafia's Chevy Revolution Tour.

Here I am with my buddy Larry the Cable Guy; and my good friend and date for the night, Miss Indiana 2008, Brittany Mason; at the Murat Theatre in Indianapolis.

I was thrilled to be able to introduce my mom and dad to Larry the Cable Guy. My mom talked quite a while about how great a time they had! This was just a year before Mom passed away.

Fan Becky Snider of Longview, Texas, and me. This time I'm on the other side of the meet-and-greet.

You will probably recognize the General Lee from *The Dukes of Hazzard*. After meeting lots of my entertainment heroes, this was and still is one of my favorites!

My new friend, Joel Osteen, and me before a live presentation of his in Nashville in 2011.

The infamous George Lindsey (Goober Pyle from *The Andy Griffith Show*) and me at a Larry the Cable Guy Christmas show taping.

Dave Ramsey and me on a private jet, ready to go to the live broadcast finale of *The Celebrity Apprentice*.

The Nashville crew at the finale of *The Celebrity Apprentice* with my friends Kelly Lang, Dave Ramsey, Sharon Ramsey, winner John Rich, and Ronnie Barrett.

few drinks I leaned back thinking I was near a wall and instead fell backward off my scooter. Unfortunately, most bars have concrete floors. I am sure I have had more than one concussion that I don't know about. It is just through God's grace that I never hurt myself more seriously.

I also approached someone in Vegas who looked like a hooker and backpedaled really fast when I realized she wasn't. It was about this same time period when I smoked my first little bit of pot.

■ ■ ■

NONE OF THESE incidents, however, was enough to get me to quit paying for sex, drinking, or gambling. Not just yet.

As soon as we got home, I headed to a nearby riverboat casino that had opened a few years earlier. I hoped to make up the money I had lost in Vegas, but that night I lost another grand off my credit card. I went a few more times and each time I lost money. It was a demoralizing and disgusting feeling and I began gambling bigger and bigger amounts until it completely consumed me.

As you can imagine, I was stressed to the max. To break the tension and get my mind off things for a few hours I visited a strip bar in Muncie several times. I also found myself going to the south side of Indianapolis to a big strip bar there.

I liked that this bar often let me use their VIP room for couch dances. But, instead of relieving tension, these visits just grew my obsession with a woman's touch. The situation progressed and I was going to places where I paid top price to get a VIP room. The old saying that "it happens in the champagne room" is very true. However, I still had not yet had intercourse.

Even while I was visiting the strip bars, the experience was a catch-22. I felt good—really good—in the moment, but then I was overwhelmed with guilt about spending money that I didn't have on something I knew I shouldn't be doing. Most of the costs I added to the growing mountain of debt that I had on my credit cards. At several hundred dollars per visit, it wore heavily on my conscience.

I have to add that if I was pursuing a woman, my visits to the strip clubs dramatically lessened. Then, when I was rejected—which happened all the time—I'd go back to the strip clubs. One of the advantages for me was that in a strip club you are never rejected, because the almighty dollar speaks volumes. The knowledge that I was not going to be rejected fueled my desire for more visits.

Between visits to the strip clubs and running Fred N' Toby's, I still found time to gamble. As most gambling addicts know, the motive for gambling eventually changes from getting rich to breaking even. Eventually I realized that neither was going to happen. I wasn't going to make money, nor was I going to get back what I had lost. Finally, after I maxed out all my credit cards with no plan for repayment, something clicked inside of me that told me to stop gambling, and I did. Well, almost. The big black cloud involving that vice lessened, because I always knew if I kept going it would eventually ruin me.

The reason I said the vice lessened rather than stopped was that I was still "playing" with stock options, which is its own form of gambling. Sadly, I invested thirty thousand dollars from a line of credit that was meant for the restaurant. This was in the early days of the Internet bubble and of course when all that blew up, so did my thirty grand. Mom stepped in and covered my losses, enabling me by not holding me accountable. In fact, I'm not sure Dad ever knew anything about it. I guess if he didn't he does now. I hope he understands my goal was to right the many wrongs I felt I had created.

Looking back, Mom was an unwitting enabler for me. She probably should have let me crash and burn, but if she let that happen then she would have crashed and burned too. Thirty thousand is a lot to lose no matter who you are. From that experience I learned to be accountable for my actions (for the time being) and the gambling valve shut off.

To this day we perform at a lot of casinos around the country, and I think my early experience with gambling was God's way of teaching me a strong lesson. Otherwise, I might still be gambling away all the merchandise money that I earn every night. Once in a while I will play, but I hold myself to a low limit. In the more than one hundred and fifty casinos that we've performed in I've gambled maybe a dozen times. Like most addicts, my addiction went from gambling to something else. That's why I think I was able to quit gambling, because as you'll read, the addiction shifted to work, and, of course, there were still the strip bars.

■　■　■

I WAS TWENTY-SIX when I finally had intercourse and lost my virginity. I still owned Fred N' Toby's and one day another customer changed my life. This charming, beautiful lady was in her fifties and by herself. She had large, fake breasts; a ton of personality; and a lot of sexual appeal. In fact, she looked a little like the movie star Rita Hayworth. I spoke with the woman for a while and discovered she was passing through town as part of a sales job and had been through a rough divorce from an abusive man.

She hung out for a while, had a bit to drink, and we became very flirtatious with each other. When she left, I followed her to her car and asked if I could come to her hotel room. She explained that she was busy that night, but that maybe the next night.

True to her word, the next day she came in for dinner and I later followed her back to her hotel. I was giddy with anticipation and had even brought some condoms. It hadn't been discussed, but I just knew we would have sex. And we did. After, she helped me get dressed, and we talked for a while.

Looking back, there are many things about my experiences with women that I no longer pursue. Nevertheless, at the time (and for some time to come) lust, alcohol, and money were my idols, and these were the most important things in my life to pursue. From my perspective back then, I would be lying if I said I regretted that experience. I am grateful for it. I had no nervousness and the intense chemistry between us told me it was meant to happen. I am so glad that she walked into my restaurant.

■ ■ ■

BACK IN THE real world the bars, drinking, gambling, and occasional pot had my life headed down a really bad road. One night after work I had my usual meal, a slab of our signature prime rib covered in A1. sauce along with more Crown and Cokes than I can remember. I drove home completely inebriated. In truth, I'm not sure how I managed to get home without hurting myself or someone else. In the middle of the night I threw up over the side of my bed and the next morning Mom came in. She saw my mess and in a firm but concerned voice asked questions such as, "What the hell did you do last night? How did you get home? If you were drunk, how did your van get in the driveway?" That was a wake-up call for me because all of my answers were tied to who I had become and not who I truly was. I began to see my life for the enormous hot mess it really was.

The demands of the restaurant business, the never-ending battles with my parents, and life in general had me so beat up that I thought I was having a nervous breakdown. I needed someone to talk to. I needed help. I never got to the point that I actually held a loaded gun to my head, but I fantasized about it. I also thought about driving off a bridge, running out into traffic, or finding another way to die—such as intentionally contracting AIDS or getting shot. I thought about the aftermath as well, the people who would miss me, the people I would be letting down by checking out early, and even about the kind of party my friends and family would throw for me when I was gone. Does that mean I was suicidal? I don't know. But I do know that I was at a place in my life that I don't ever want to be again.

Enter Dr. Ken Barnes. Dr. Barnes, a psychologist, probably saved my life as I began seeing him for what I now understand was a deep level of depression. I was still so gregarious that being depressed was the last thing I would have thought of. With Dr. Barnes's therapy and an antidepressant that Dr. Blaisedell prescribed, my thoughts of "checking out" early turned around. I slowly regained my ability to see things from the right perspective and was able to focus on and isolate my individual problems and deal with each one head-on.

About that same time, the ongoing conversation I had been having with my parents and talks with the bank that held the mortgage on the restaurant came to a head. It brought me to the conclusion that something needed to give. Around this same time I had an offer from a local guy who inquired about leasing my restaurant for a second location in his chain of Mexican restaurants. This perception of a clean "out" allowed my pride to do what my mind had known needed to be done for some time, and that was to close the restaurant that had been my life for the past three and a half years. It was time to move on.

You might think I was devastated by the decision, but the reality was that it was a huge relief. On October 21, 2000, a Saturday night, I knew we would not be opening back up that coming Monday. That Sunday, I visited the senior staff, Chef Kevin, my administrative assistant, Mikey, Inge, and a few others at their homes to deliver the news in person and offer them severance pay. They knew there had been problems, but I wore the mask of stability so well that no one realized we were in as bad a shape as we were.

■ ■ ■

IN THE THREE and a half years I operated Fred N' Toby's, a lifetime of lessons had been acquired. Some of those lessons stuck, others I repeated several times over. A few I am still repeating. One popular definition of insanity is doing the same thing over and over again and expecting a different result. I do keep that in mind.

One of the lessons that stuck was about finding people's strengths and then letting them run with it. By the time Fred N' Toby's closed, Toby had graduated from Ball State and had been working at the restaurant for about six months. I know now it was not his thing and he probably knew then but never spoke up.

Kix Brooks (of the former mega country duo Brooks & Dunn) once told me about a conversation he had with his dad about chopping wood. His dad was talking about buying a log splitter to make the job easier. Kix mentioned that what would be even easier yet would be to buy the wood already split. His dad stopped and looked at Kix and then said something to the effect of, "Son, when you are my age you look at two things when you purchase something. One, do you want it, and two, can you pay cash for it." In other words Kix's dad had earned the right to do and spend what he wanted.

I feel that way about Toby. He loves fishing and sports. I hope someday soon he can combine those passions with his career. If that's what he wants to do, then I will help and support him in any way I can, just as he did for my dream and me.

The biggest lesson of all of this is that Fred N' Toby's was financially not too bad off. It was the expansions and closings of the other ventures that brought everything down.

13

THE HURDLES
OF DAILY LIFE

In the middle of all of the restaurant chaos, in true Fred fashion I made time to get my real estate salesperson's license and then got my broker's license. How I fit all of this in, I have no idea. Less than a month after closing the restaurant I spearheaded creating an organization (which included Toby, Mom, and Dad) called Gill Enterprises, LLC. The first thing we did was purchase a small house that served as our office. At first Toby and I manned the office, but we soon hired my childhood friend Angie Champ (now Angie Fletcher) to be our leasing agent. We also hired a maintenance man. Toby did the books and my dad was also involved in the business, so it was once again a family affair.

Of course, once again I dove in deep too fast. (Remember the definition of insanity?) My immediate goal was to purchase five hundred residential rental units. Five hundred! What was I thinking? Money, money, money. That's exactly what I was thinking. Within eighteen months I was more than halfway to my goal, having acquired two hundred fifty-nine. Strategically, most of them were located within five minutes of the office.

My business model was to buy a property for less than the appraised value, then make sure it appraised for well above the purchase price. After I made an extremely small escrow payment and bought the property, there was usually cash out at closing. We'd take the cash we got back at closing and put it into our business. What we were doing was not illegal, but it is what brought down the real estate market on a national level a few years later. Because everyone was doing this, the market became overinflated and then crashed.

We got mortgages on all of the properties and also used equity on properties Mom and Dad had owned for years and had paid for with cash. To say that I was overleveraged is an understatement. For as long as I could remember my goal was to be a millionaire by the time I was thirty, and on paper, I had achieved that goal. At the height of our real estate boom our company was worth fifteen million, but ten million of that was debt. The way I come to my millionaire status is: five million divided by four people is 1.25 million—on paper. We had zero liquidity, which meant we truly had a house of cards.

Toby and I lived very frugally but it still wasn't enough. It took ten years for all of it to come crashing down, versus the three and a half years I was in the restaurant business. To be fair, many of the problems we ended up having with the real estate company were due to the economy, and the real estate and mortgage bust that began around 2007 and came to a head in 2009.

Like a lot of businesses, our company was a reflection of the times. Even if I had been astute enough to have an inkling of the coming real estate crash (which very few did), my parents were so against change that I probably would not have been able to do anything about it inside of our company. For example, they had a hard time with simple changes that interrupted their daily routine. If that situation had been different, we would have gotten out a lot sooner, and a lot cleaner. Hindsight, as they say.

I do know that when I was in high school and college I had no idea that my dream of being an entrepreneur would be so frustrating and challenging . . . and yes, rewarding, all at the same time. When a person is young, they tend to have a glowing image of what their dreams and goals should look like. I never envisioned any of these entrepreneurial challenges when I was thinking about my dream. If I had, then maybe I would have been better equipped to deal with them or would have avoided them altogether. I now know that to succeed in life you have to fail many times. I had lessons to learn through each challenge and there was a good reason God put all He did in my path.

In the meantime, the lease had run out on the building that used to be Fred N' Toby's and the man who ran the Mexican restaurant was not going to renew the contract. It was difficult in a small town to sell an older building that was set up for a specific use and come out ahead, or break even. So, we now had a potentially empty building on our hands for which we had to come up with a monthly mortgage payment.

Toby and I were wrapped up in the real estate business and I knew I didn't have the mental or financial capacity to go back into the restaurant business. We kicked around a few things and I finally said to Mom, Dad, and Toby, "How about a bar?" Just a bar. There would be no full-scale kitchen or a full waitstaff, and the profit from the business would only have to pay the note and building upkeep. It took some discussion and a little more money. Both involved Mom and Dad.

After the initial anxiety of getting back into something that previously had been a nightmare, everyone was excited about the idea. We began throwing around some names for the new bar. One day during a family dinner I caught the credits of a *Wheel of Fortune* episode and saw the word "monk." I began mouthing the words, "Monk, Monk, Funkey Monk." When I got to Funkey Monkey Toby said, "Done."

The transition was very easy, especially compared to the first time around. The building and liquor license had stayed in our name, so there were no problems on that end. We spent about fifteen thousand dollars turning the inside from a Mexican place into a pub, hired two or three people to staff the place, and in just a few weeks we were in business.

It was so much easier running the Funkey Monkey than it was Fred N' Toby's. First and foremost, the hours I spent there were limited and were by my choice. Also, with the restaurant we had been open from eleven A.M. until past midnight. With the pub we didn't open until four in the afternoon.

Another good thing was that the Monkey required a mere percentage of the staff we used to have. It is a lot easier to manage three people than it is thirty. And it was convenient for me. I always had a place to drink free. By this time, with the help of Dr. Barnes and the meds, I was not nearly as out of control as I had once been. But I wasn't where I needed to be in terms of drinking in moderation.

The Funkey Monkey did as well as it needed to for several years—until the city decided to put in the new Seymour Police Department just across the street. Somehow the patrons of our beer-slinging, whiskey-pouring bar no longer felt comfortable on our stools with so many law enforcement personnel just a few steps away. Business dropped off dramatically, but we hung in there for a while and survived on event-driven business such as Seymour's annual Oktoberfest. I wasn't worried, however, as the apartments were keeping us busy enough.

■ ■ ■

ABOUT THIS TIME my parents took Grandma and Grandpa Wilson to Wisconsin one last time. This was their fiftieth visit. When I think of it, I am still amazed by the marriage they had and the marriage Grandma and Grandpa Gill had. My parents' marriage, too. People just don't stay together anymore like that. I wish they did, and when it comes time I intend to as well.

Grandpa Gill was my first grandparent to, as my friend Joel Osteen says of his father, "go to be with the Lord." He had been in bad shape for the previous seven years due to a series of strokes, and while his passing on was very sad, I knew it was a natural part of life. Grandma took care of Grandpa all those years that he was bedridden, but as of the writing of this book she recently celebrated her ninety-fifth birthday. She is still sharp and going strong.

Grandpa Wilson passed January 12, 2003, and Grandma passed in December of that year. The last time our family went to

Wisconsin, we went without Grandma and Grandpa Wilson and we stayed in a hotel instead of a cabin. We took my friend Bubba with us, but it wasn't the same, and that's the last time I was there. In times of extreme stress, like the night I crawled under my desk to hide from the world, I fantasize about just taking off and driving to the comfort and safety of the cabin on South Two Lake or the darkness of Wind Pudding Lake.

I am so fortunate to have had my grandparents in my life for so long; they all are a big part of who I am today. But I remember the losses not fully sinking in until much later. During the services of both Grandma and Grandpa Wilson I was in pursuit of girls and was distracted from my mourning by waiting for the next text message to come in. It was not an intentional thing at the time, to not deal with the passing of these people who meant so much to me. Rather, it was all about my addictive personality, which, in addition to gambling and alcohol, also fixated on women.

■ ■ ■

BUSINESS STRESSES ASIDE, some good things were happening, too. During the restaurant years, I purchased a house in the same neighborhood we grew up in. It was a brick ranch with a great floor plan. Toby lived with me and we were just a block over from Mom and Dad, but the cool thing was the house was mine!

I especially liked the fact that I could set up a woodworking shop in the one-car garage that wasn't big enough for my truck. Working with wood and building things had been a hobby of mine since I was a child. As needed, I built devices to adapt tools I used so they worked for me. If I couldn't grip something hard enough, then maybe I could add length to the tool so I could leverage it better. I also set up my own tools at my level, just like I needed them, and also had room to have several projects going at once. And, just as I did when I was a kid, I also took many things apart with no intent of ever putting them back together again. Of course, I didn't have a lot of time to spend on my hobby, but when I did, it was a great stress reliever and took my mind off the troubles I had at work.

As great as home ownership was, it presented an obvious problem. I still could not go to the bathroom by myself, and dressing was still very difficult. Toby is more limber than I am and was dressing independently in college, so it wasn't as much of an issue for him. Toby, however, could not physically help me much so I had to figure out a way very quickly.

Backing up to my childhood, Mom hated the word "poop." Instead, she always asked if we had to "go sit." So in that way in our house, just like the word "poop," "sit" was used as both a verb and a noun. To this day I think in my brain that I have to go sit. We also used the word "tinkle" instead of another euphemism, such as "potty" or "pee." Way into my twenties I "tinkled." Yeah, yeah, I know.

I remember a time back in college when the "sitting" situation came to a head. I was Christmas-shopping with Kristi Grinstead at the Greenwood Mall and had to use the bathroom. Typically, if I was out and about I had a guy friend with me who could help, but that was not the case on this particular day. I had to pee badly and there was no buddy to assist me. The help I needed was as simple as zipping up my jeans. If I needed assistance today, I would ask the female friend I was with, but back then I was way too anxious about these matters to do that.

Instead, after I did my business I wrestled my pants up as best I could, then swallowed my pride and asked a total stranger who happened to be in the bathroom to zip and snap my jeans. Talk about big-time embarrassment; this was it, front and center. The poor guy was about as nervous as I was, but I am grateful to this day for his help.

Then something amazing happened. I had always worn jeans off the rack that Mom converted to fit me, but the zippers, buttons, and snap closures were impossible for me to deal with. I realized that switching to khaki pants with an elastic waistband would change my life. With the elastic waist, I could push the front of my pants down by putting my cane inside my pants. Then I could lean over, urinate, and use the cane to pull my pants back up again.

By the time I had moved out of my parents' home, I had figured out a system of having Mom sew loops on the sides of my pants and underwear so I could use an extra set of canes as arm extensions to pull my pants and underwear up. If I was in public it was as simple as using my walking sticks and pulling the rubber tips off.

But "sitting" was another matter altogether. How would I not only get my underwear and pants back up but wipe my own bottom? Up to this point, someone else had to do this for me.

During the process of moving into my new house, I had another amazing revelation. Using maintenance men from our business, I had the bathroom altered so it was built up around the tub and toilet. That way it was at a level that Toby and I could use. I then had the idea of putting an old milk crate in the corner by the toilet. Then I used my cane to get my pants and underwear off and did my business. After I was done, I put a double layer of wet wipes on the corner of the crate, sat on them, and wiggled.

It worked! You have no idea how liberating it is for me to wipe my own butt. I could hardly believe I could finally "sit" by myself! I didn't need someone to assist me several times a day. I didn't need to be dependent physically on anyone. For me, this was an even bigger accomplishment than getting my van and learning to drive. It was the most life-changing thing I'd ever done. So far.

Becoming independent in the bathroom wasn't all smooth sailing, though. Often, it was a slow progression and a true struggle. There were times I got very frustrated and I remember being on the road one hot and sticky summer day when it took me a full twenty minutes just to get my underwear on after a shower. Those kinds of situations are so aggravating to me, and not only because they are time-consuming, but because they are physically demanding as well.

It took me a long time to fully realize the enormity of the freedom being independent in the bathroom allowed. I think the biggest advantage of it is that it shaped my innate ability to be prepared—for anything.

Today I carry wet wipes with me all the time. At home I also have a small polyurethane box that I use in the bathroom. It works well, is easy to clean, and is sanitary. I also carry a similar

THE HURDLES OF DAILY LIFE

box with me in my scooter. So if you have ever wondered how Two Foot Fred wipes his own butt, now you know.

■ ■ ■

NOW THAT I was fully independent, I began fine-tuning other areas of self-sufficiency. If I couldn't reach a breaker box, for example, rather than call someone I figured out a way to use my sticks to flip the breaker myself. In case a home or business I needed to enter didn't have a scooter-accessible entrance for my scooter, I worked on increasing my walking skills. Walking is difficult because my scoliosis surgery changed the shape of my body so much that my balance is completely off. Trouble taking out the trash? I used smaller bags. I definitely live by the motto "If there is a will, there is a way."

While I was thrilled with all that I could now do on my own, at the same time I was disappointed that Mom did not help Toby and me learn these things—and many others—when we were much younger. Why did she not better prepare us for life? For living on our own? There is no reason I could not have had trash duty when I was in high school or used the toilet independently before my middle twenties. I loved my mom, but I came to the conclusion that she was an enabler in this area, just as much as she was in bailing me out of my gambling debts and business situations.

Now that I have had several years of off-and-on therapy and have matured more, I better understand that we all have parents who have their own troubles and backgrounds and emotional issues. Mom's was that she needed to be needed. By unknowingly keeping Toby and me reliant upon her, she was able to obtain the feeling of validation.

Mom aside, now that Toby and I were living on our own, exercising and eating healthily presented some of our biggest difficulties. Mom and Dad had gotten bicycles for Toby and me sometime after Fred N' Toby's closed. I used to ride mine furiously around the neighborhood to work off some of my frustration. Two times around the big outer block was a mile. Now I struggled to find the time and energy.

I was not as health-conscious then as I am now, and cooking was often not an option. Toby and I often did what we could with a frozen meal or a flat-topped griddle on which we made our specialty, grilled cheese.

Although it does not have much to do with independence, it was also frustrating for me at this time in my life to deal with people who, seeing my shortened stature, assumed that I was also short on brains. Long ago I had learned to tune most of that out. In fact, whenever I was out with friends, they noticed it far more than I did, but the occasional rude person broke through my radar.

I always handled these situations in the best way I knew how. First I'd flash my big Fred smile and try to engage them in conversation. If that worked, then just by talking with me they quickly realized I was as intelligent as they were, if not more so. Some people, though, did not respond well to my overtures and many times I wrote them off as not worth it.

That is, I wrote them off until the day I had a chance encounter that I now realize was divine in nature; it was a God moment. One of many I have had in my life. When I was in high school a guy came to fix our pool. We had gotten a fiberglass in-ground pool when I was about fifteen. It was a big pool, one piece, with steps all the way across the shallow end. Toby and I swam a lot in it and one day at the deep end one of us noticed a crack in the bottom of the pool.

The pool had a lifetime warranty so we called the company that installed it and they sent a subcontractor out to repair it. Fixing a crack in a pool like that is kind of tricky, because you can't drain it. If you do, you risk the chance that the changing pressure caused by the receding water will pop the pool right out of the ground. A skilled technician has to make the repair underwater.

The guy who showed up was unimposing, to say the least. I was on the back porch tweaking the handlebars on my scooter, and we talked as he laid out his scuba gear on the picnic table I was using as a workbench. I was pretty interested his homemade scuba equipment, and in the man, who was wiry and scruffy and had several tattoos. If I'd seen him on the side of the road, I would have assumed he was a drifter.

But as we talked, I quickly realized he was a soft-spoken, kind, and gentle soul who was getting his degree in theology. Back then I didn't have a clear idea what theology was, and this man didn't look like he was about to get a degree in anything, much less a subject that had to do with God.

The more I think about it, the more I realize this truly was a God moment. It took me many years to process and understand that I received a huge lesson in judgment. I realized that someone might judge me without taking the time to know me, but I was doing the same to other people. I had no way of knowing what was in that person's background that made them look or act a certain way. Who knows what difficulties, what challenges, they had to deal with in their life?

I was disappointed to discover that I had judged this man on the basis of his looks, just as people had often judged me. I, who was the first to shout loud and clear that you can't assume anything from looking at a person, had done just that. After this realization, once I stopped judging others, I found that I stopped noticing others judging me. I didn't understand then that God is our only judge, and God used this man to help me come to that realization on my own.

14

PURSUING MY
PASSION WITH PASSION

Growing up, other than watching the television show *Hee Haw*, which was a Saturday night staple in our home, I was not a huge fan of country music, or any music other than what was played on the radio when I rode in a car.

The other show we watched on occasion on Saturday nights, especially with Grandma and Grandpa Wilson, was *The Lawrence Welk Show* on PBS. For Toby and me this old-time musical variety show was torture, but we wanted to spend time with Grandma and Grandpa, so we suffered through it.

By the time I had my DJ business in high school, I was mostly into Top Forty pop music. I made sure to play whatever the kids attending the dance most wanted to hear, because my success and popularity as a DJ depended on keeping kids out on the dance floor. I mostly played current pop songs, but once in a while I'd get a request for something by Garth Brooks, such as

"Friends in Low Places," or "Boot Scootin' Boogie" by Brooks & Dunn, or the Alison Krauss version of "When You Say Nothing at All." Later, "Achy Breaky Heart" by Billy Ray Cyrus was such a smash that every DJ had it in their library, including me. That was the extent of my knowledge of the country music genre.

Like most college freshmen in the mid-1990s, I made mix tapes. These were cassette tapes of songs I liked and sometimes recorded from the radio. Back then only a few songs were available as cassette singles, so I didn't think there was anything wrong with recording something from the radio, especially as I was only a Top Forty listener.

On one of those tapes was the Toby Keith song "Should've Been a Cowboy." There were a few other country songs on there, too, but my interest was more situational to a specific song rather than to the entire genre. Before too long, however, the country influence in my life began to grow.

My roommate Mike Sutton confided to me that he had secretly begun listening to a country station in his car. One day he came home and said, "You have to listen to this song, it's awesome." The tune was "Dust on the Bottle" by David Lee Murphy, and the song blew me away. I couldn't get enough of it. Another roommate, Chad Huddleston, was crazy about Hootie and the Blowfish, but then again, who wasn't? While that band was not country per se, their lead singer, Darius Rucker, is now one of the hottest male solo artists in the genre.

During our junior year our house listened to a lot of diverse music, which included the country super-band Alabama. One of us heard that Alabama was going to perform on campus at Ball State University's Worthen Arena, and we knew we had to go.

There was also a bonus factor in that Neal McCoy was going to open for them, and he had a song out that I liked.

Earlier in my life, the last thing I thought I'd ever do was go to a country music concert. But I am so glad that I went. Neal turned out to be an awesome entertainer, and Alabama performed all of their megahits that we sang along to in our house every day. After that I was hooked. I started listening to country music more and began learning who the individual artists were.

As a side note, Darius Rucker is now one of my better friends in the industry, and I hang out as much as I can with country star Toby Keith whenever we are in the same location at the same time. Also interesting, a man named Dale Morris managed Alabama and one of his partners, Marc Oswald, also worked with the band. Today, Marc manages the group I tour with, Big & Rich, under the Dale Morris umbrella, which is now under the umbrella of Irving Azoff's entertainment empire. Full circle? You tell me.

Back in the Gilly's pizza days, our manager, Terry Whipple, turned me on to a young female country singer named Chely Wright. I began watching her, and other artists, on the cable channels CMT (Country Music Television) and TNN (The Nashville Network). Then I learned that Chely was going to perform at the Little Nashville Opry in Nashville, Indiana. That was only forty-five minutes from Seymour!

After watching Chely's performance, my mind kicked into gear. I wanted to get a country artist to perform in the parking lot at Fred N' Toby's. The restaurant itself was far too small to do an indoor concert of that magnitude, but outside, that was a different story. I did some research and came up with two booking agencies: William Morris (now William Morris Endeavor) and CAA (Creative Artists Agency), two of the country's top agencies. Jeff Hill at CAA was the first to return my phone call and he worked diligently to find an artist that would fit our small venue. CAA worked with a then-rising star named Shane Minor and suggested he might be the right guy for my event.

This was the first time I had ever dealt with an artist rider, and I was nervous that we wouldn't have enough towels or the right brand of other things the rider required. Most artists include on their rider (which is an attachment to the performance contract) things they need in their dressing room or after the show, such as specific kinds of food, beverages, towels, et cetera. Some artists have rider requirements that are outrageous, but I was fortunate that Jeff Hill assured me that Shane would not be too concerned about the small things in the rider.

I had a large vehicle, so I designated myself as runner for the show. This meant I was the one who drove everyone to and from places they needed to go. It was an important position on several levels. First, because artists usually come in on a bus, it is hard for them to travel locally, such as to and from the hotel or, if needed, to Wal-Mart for supplies. Second, it allowed me to meet Shane and his entourage and talk with them one-on-one, so I got to learn more about them and their lives in the entertainment business. I thought it was all pretty cool.

The only snafu I had was that Shane's road manager was a stickler for detail and it took Shane, who is a great people person, stepping in a few times to smooth everything over.

The other unforgettable person I met was Chief. He was a

big, round guy who was driving Shane's bus and who also had driven Garth Brooks's bus for Garth's entire career. I was more than thrilled to hear stories about Garth when I taxied Chief to and from the hotel. After the show, Shane, the band, and the crew ate dinner with us at the restaurant and hung out for quite a while.

After that, I went to see Shane perform at the Little Nashville Opry. An added bonus was that Chely Wright was opening for Shane. Shane got me an all-access pass and I was hanging out with him backstage when one of Chely's band members did a last-minute check in the mirror. When he was done, I said, "Have a great show, man." He gave me a friendly smile and a wave as he walked onstage.

I now know that man was Jay DeMarcus. He and another member of Chely's band, Joe Don Rooney, went on to become two of three members of one of country music's most celebrated groups, Rascal Flatts.

Life really is all about relationships. Today, Jay and his wife, Tiffany, and Joe Don and his wife, Allison, are friends I see frequently in Nashville.

■ ■ ■

BY SPRING OF 1999, I'd been in the restaurant business a little less than two years and as you already know, I was completely burned out. I was sitting on my parents' back porch smoking a cigar one evening, trying to de-stress from whatever the day's fiasco had been at the restaurant. I was frustrated with work and with life in general. For once, I didn't know what to do.

I have recently realized that I am an idea guy and I need people to implement the many ideas I come up with. I need doers. After a lot of therapy and self-reflection I have also realized there is nothing wrong with that. That I need doers is not only due to my stature, which renders some tasks physically difficult, or even impossible, but also because of the way my brain works. I am a starter. I have a talent for creating the idea and also for putting the idea into place, but I need doers to keep the idea going.

For the most part we had great staff at the restaurant, but for some reason my "doers" weren't doing enough. Not yet knowing any of the above, I put the blame on me and had worn myself out physically and mentally thinking about changes to our business strategies, staffing, and overall operations.

Then I remembered seeing or hearing something about this thing in Nashville called Fan Fair. This was a big country music event that was held in Nashville annually in June. This four-day extravaganza put the stars of country music in direct contact with their fans through autograph signings, concerts, meet-and-greets, contests, and other fun activities. I already had major cash-flow problems and certainly did not have the money to just up and go to Nashville, but I needed some space. I bought a ticket to the event on my credit card anyway.

Not knowing how far out it was from the fairgrounds in Nashville, I stayed at the Holiday Inn in Brentwood, some ten miles south of town. Other than the extreme, unbearable heat in the barns at the Nashville fairgrounds where the stars were signing autographs, the entire event was great. I met some really cool people that I remain friends with to this day. Plus, the concerts in the evening were amazing, and I knew I'd be back the next year.

■ ■ ■

THE FIRST TIME I went to Fan Fair I was at a huge crossroads in my life. I was running from the issues at home and wondering how—or if—I'd get out of the hole I was digging for my family and myself with the restaurants and other failures. To take this unaffordable trip seemed counterproductive, but it was something I knew in my gut I had to do. Now I understand it was divine intervention.

After the trip, I knew I had to do more than just run my existing businesses and battle depression. One thing that came to mind was an idea I'd been tossing around for some time for a spice product, Phat Freddie's Seasonings. It tied in well with the restaurant business but was unique enough to challenge my creativity and meet my need to always be starting something.

Like many restaurant owners, I took my main meal between two and five in the afternoon, when the kitchen was quiet. Our chef had a six-foot spice rack, and I started playing around with different mixes to put on the steak while it was cooking. Eventually I came up with one that I loved and that everyone else liked as well.

My goal for the spices was that they be sold on QVC and I knew that because of price points QVC would not sell just one bottle of seasoning. With that in mind I blended three more flavors and added a bottle of pure granulated garlic and one of pure granulated onion for a six-pack of great seasonings. My spices are quality all-natural products that have no fillers or preservatives added. If you want more information on them, go to www.twofootfred.com.

After quite a few test runs I took my idea and recipes to

Marion-Kay Spices in Brownstown, Indiana, a boutique supplier of high-end spices to the food industry. Brownstown is only ten minutes from Seymour, and I worked with John Reid, a grandson of the company's founder, to fine-tune my mix and create a mass-production formula.

For whatever reason, even though John was interested in manufacturing my spice line, we never went any further than discussion. However, a few years later I decided to again pursue development and this time worked with John's son Scott.

I have mentioned several times how important relationships are, and this is a prime example. Scott Reid just happened to have been my orientation leader at Ball State University and was a senior when I was a freshman. It definitely pays to completely connect with people who come into your life, as you never know when they might reappear.

I was excited to be working with Scott, because he saw the vision much the same way I did. With Scott's passion for the development side of the business (and as my point person), we worked well together in moving forward. After we finished the packaging design and a small run of samples, I was all set to present Phat Freddie's at one of QVC's open calls in Birmingham, Alabama.

God, however, had different plans for me. Around that same time the e-mail came in from John Rich about appearing in the "Save a Horse (Ride a Cowboy)" video. Fortunately, QVC held their last open call the weekend after we shot the video. It meant five extra hours of driving, but I was there. I later received a letter that said QVC wanted to sell my product, but then my buyer, the person who was in charge of the food department, changed, as did the next one, and the one after that. Apparently Phat Freddie's and QVC were not meant to be at that particular time. Someday soon I will get back to the spices. They really are good and I'd love to share them with people across the country, including you.

■ ■ ■

ALTHOUGH I DIDN'T know it at the time, my second year at Fan Fair was going to be a life-changing experience. From the previous year, I'd learned a few things about the event and this time chose to stay downtown at the Sheraton Hotel. That way I could ride my scooter all over town and hit all the clubs and parties that were going on after events at the fairgrounds were over.

One of the many people I met when I was out and about was a guy named Sam, who was a bouncer at the famous Wildhorse Saloon on Second Avenue. He said if I waited until his shift at the Wildhorse was over, he'd take me down to the Beer Sellar, a pub where a lot of locals hung out, including some from the music industry.

The next night I went back on my own and that was when I met the man who changed the course of my life forever, John Rich. John had been the co–lead singer and bass player for a band called Lonestar that was beginning to have quite a bit of success. That success created differences between John and the rest of the band and he left. John then started a solo career and had a single out on BNA Records called "I Pray for You." By that time my finger was on the pulse of everything that was happening in country music, including knowing who John was.

John was easy to spot with his trademark mustache, and I

motioned him over to my barstool. We talked about music and his career as he waited for his girlfriend, who was a waitress at the pub. John, of course, was not nearly at the level of stardom that he is now, but I still thought it was cool that we seemed to hit it off from a conversational standpoint. We also connected again later that night at Legends Corner. By that time John had then-budding artist Keith Anderson with him, whom I quickly became friends with as well. I am proud that Keith remains one of my very good Nashville friends.

The next day at Fan Fair I ended up in the BNA Records autograph line, and to my surprise, there again was John. When he signed his name to the back of a glossy photo of himself, he also wrote down his e-mail address and asked me to stay in touch. I was elated that he would do something like that, but I have come to learn that's just who John is.

That same Fan Fair I met a lot of big country music artists. Many of the stars had special handicapped lines that I could zip into to avoid wait times that sometimes ran six hours or more. One of the lines I stumbled into was that of Tim McGraw and Faith Hill. I remember that Tim said, in reference to my scooter, "Hey, man, I like your Harley," and I came right back with, "Yeah, but it's not a horse." This was right after the incident where he and Kenny Chesney jumped on the back of a police horse and rode it across the parking lot at one of their shows. It was all in good fun, but they both got into a lot of trouble for it. However, the exposure, good or bad, helped both of their careers.

I also met Neal McCoy, whom I had become a fan of in college; LeAnn Rimes; and the Warren Brothers, among others. In another ironic full circle thing, in just a few short years, McGraw,

John Rich and Big Kenny, the Warren Brothers, and I would all be out on tour together.

I went to Fan Fair, which now is called the CMA Music Festival, two or three years in a row. I was too busy to go in 2003, and little did I know that when I attended in 2004, I'd be behind the scenes with my favorite artists. I have attended every CMA Fest since, only now from the other side of the fence, which is pretty wild.

■　■　■

BY THIS TIME the old blue and white van that I'd had for so many years had been "rode hard and put away wet" too many times and the repair issues were never-ending. It was time to get a newer vehicle. After several conversations with Bruce Ahnafield of the Ahnafield Corporation about how I didn't want another van, he believed he could convert a Suburban. My search began for the perfect vehicle, and I found a black 2002 Chevy suburban with the Z71 sport package that I really liked. It was calling my name.

A lot of technology had advanced since I got my first vehicle twelve years ago. With the van, the object had been to bring the controls to me by adding extensions onto most of the levers and making the switches remote. The Suburban was already designed like a cockpit where everything was closer to the driver, and with a simple back cushion I sat farther forward in the seat. With this design I did not need the six-way swivel seat or other extensions and remotes that were necessary in the van. I can easily get from my scooter to the slightly raised driver's seat. And once in the seat I only need the forward-and-back adjustment that is typical of most powered car seats. A simple relocation of those controls was all that it took.

Instead of the drawbridge, or platform lift, that I had on the van, I now had an under-vehicle lift (UVL). The difference is that the drawbridge lift is located inside the van's rear passenger-side double doors. After the doors are opened the platform folds out of the van. While effective, it takes up a lot of space, weighs a ton, and is unsightly.

A UVL lift is mounted underneath the vehicle and remains out of sight and out of the way until it is needed. This makes it easier for passengers to get in the rear of the vehicle and allows for more space inside.

The rest of the Z71 conversion included pedal extensions, a small steering wheel, a customized driver's seat-back cushion, and the removal of the center console, which was replaced by a solid carpeted box. Because the middle seat had been taken out to make room for my scooter, I had the idea to use the leather from the seat to make my seat-back cushion.

Now all I have to do is open the powered side door, lower and extend the lift, back my scooter in, raise the lift to the level of the Suburban's floor, and back in behind the driver's seat. Then I take two steps on the box, turn around, and plop down into the seat. I am ready to go.

I still have the old van. It is parked in Seymour, just in case Toby or I ever need a backup. Remember, we can't just hop into any vehicle and drive. I have so many great memories of that van, so many milestones and successes, that I smile whenever I think about it. But I soon would have a lot more to smile about, and it was more than most people could ever dream of.

15

PULLING IT
ALL TOGETHER

Over the next few years, John Rich and I
e-mailed randomly a few times a year. Through those e-mails,
we were able to remain distant friends, and I thought it was cool
to know someone in the entertainment business. Long before it
was common to do so, I regularly sent e-mails to promote Fred
N' Toby's, and later the Funkey Monkey. John was on that list
and usually bounced back an e-mail with a "Hey, man, how's it
going?"

I believe it was this constant communication that had my
information at his fingertips when the time was right. When John
partnered with his best friend Big Kenny Alphin for a new duo
that would push musical boundaries, I was thrilled that he asked
me be a part of their first video, "Save a Horse (Ride a Cowboy)."

When the cameras finally stopped rolling and the circus of the
video shoot wrapped, it was time for the after-party. Then we had

an after-after-party. Only a select few went to the second party, which was held at Fontanel. I had a gut feeling that things might get a little wild, so even though I initially planned to spend that night at the hotel, I packed my bags and brought them with me. Just in case. I'm glad I did because it was a great party—so great that I ended up crashing on a couch in the "big room" at Fontanel.

I should also note that whenever I got very drunk I became less and less concerned with where I went to the bathroom. I hate to admit it, but in a crowded bar I might even pee in the corner. (Not that I remember peeing in a corner at Fontanel, but I might have.) I really had fewer challenges about using the bathroom when I was that drunk, because I cared less.

One time after I had moved to Nashville I woke up in my apartment to find that my truck, scooter, and cell phone were in three different locations. Sober, I would never leave my scooter and billfold in the hallway of a bar or leave my truck in a parking lot unlocked. But when I was drunk? That was another story. However, unlike most other people, I can't easily fix all of that. I can't just jump in someone else's car and go pick up my scooter, because not every car is large enough to carry my scooter. And, without my scooter, I can't always access places where my cell phone might be.

It was at Fontanel that I met a guy called Alaska Dan. He lived in a tent on the Fontanel property, and when everyone was passing out, myself included, he found a pillow for me and helped me onto a couch in the big room.

I remember that Dan said, "When you wake up in the morning you are going to think, 'Where in the hell am I?'" And he was absolutely right.

At that time I wore contacts and had managed to take them out. When I woke, through bleary eyes, I could not believe the enormity of the room I was in and how I got there. It was totally surreal. "Hold on," I thought, "were the last twenty-four hours a dream?" Oh no, they were real. Very real.

Dan and a girl named Elissa, who later became a friend, had attended the party and shared the room, one each on a couch on either side of me. Earlier, when I said the room was big, I mean really big—like four-thousand-square-feet big. The house also had a lot of steps, so Dan and Elissa helped me get my scooter past the barrage of steps to where my vehicle was parked.

When I got in my truck, I realized how hungover I really was. But that was balanced with a high from having shot the video. I started up, then drove back to my regular life. By "regular life" I mean that I still had apartments to buy and the Funkey Monkey to run. On the way back to Seymour I had a mounting feeling of regret that I had paid for an expensive hotel room that wasn't used. Then it hit me from a different perspective. Would I have spent the same amount of money to spend the night at Fontanel? Yes, I would have. Was that money a possible investment in future projects? Definitely.

When I got home Toby and I discussed that year's lineup for Oktoberfest for the Funkey Monkey. Because the Monkey was located in the heart of the festivities during this annual festival, we set up a beer garden and a stage in the parking lot. I asked if he thought we should bring in Big & Rich and Toby replied, "Do you think they'll be a hit?"

To me, it wasn't even a question, but then again, I had been in the middle of something he had not experienced. I felt John and

Kenny would hit it big, but I didn't have a clue as to the timeline.

■ ■ ■

BY THE TIME the CMA Music Festival rolled around in early June 2004, the video had been released and I remember being caught off guard, and yet proud, when several girls in the elevator at the Renaissance Hotel recognized me. When they asked for my autograph I wasn't expecting it. I was taken aback but at the same time I was flattered. They wanted *my* signature.

As time went on, while I subconsciously liked it, I questioned the fact that people wanted my autograph just because I was in a video. In my mind, that didn't make me worthy of signing my name to a piece of paper or a picture. Then I came to the decision that if someone wanted my autograph it was an insult to them if I didn't give it, even though I did not feel deserving—in more ways than one. I had to spend a lot of time on the road and endure countless guilty feelings before I could comfortably take the compliment of an autograph or picture request at face value and with appreciation.

Later that evening, at the big nightly concert event at LP Field, I again got to spend time with members of the MuzikMafia. We were set up outside Gretchen Wilson's bus as Gretchen performed "Redneck Woman," the song that went on to define Gretchen and her career, during Brooks & Dunn's set.

By this time I had been to two MuzikMafia shows, one in Memphis and one in Knoxville. The "Mafia" in MuzikMafia actually stands for Musically Artistic Friends in Alliance and their motto is "Music without prejudice." A Mafia show was magical and spontaneous because you never knew who would show up or what would happen.

The movement started when John and a group of fellow artists, who at the time were all down-and-out, began getting together to perform at ten P.M. on Tuesday nights in Nashville. Tuesday was chosen because it was the slowest night of the week and everyone who attended or performed had to make an effort to be there. This meant that it took a commitment to be part of the Mafia. They started at the Pub of Love, which is across the street from the bar 12th & Porter. It is located, not surprisingly, on the corner of Twelfth and Porter in downtown Nashville. The core group was John Rich, Big Kenny Alphin, Cory Gierman, Jon Nicholson, and others including Gretchen Wilson, Cowboy Troy, and James Otto.

The MuzikMafia was formed and headed by four guys we referred to as "godfathers": John, Kenny, singer/songwriter Jon Nicholson, and music publisher Cory Gierman, who handled the business side of the Mafia. Together they decided that for it to be an official Mafia one of the godfathers had to be present. While they all struggled to find their footing in the music industry, there were seventy-two Tuesday Mafias in a row.

As word spread throughout Nashville's music community, the Mafia began holding their events at larger and larger venues. Eventually label heads took note of the growing popularity and just about everyone involved either got a record deal or stepped up into a higher level of Nashville's fickle hierarchy.

Several official satellite Mafia events were also held. One that I went to in Memphis took place after a Kid Rock concert and Kid Rock stayed to play and party with the Mafia. Eventually he became an honorary member.

At the Memphis event I overheard the guys talking about a big Mafia event that was going to be held after the 2004 Academy of Country Music Awards show in Las Vegas. Big & Rich were going to make their TV debut on the show and I was thrilled when they invited me to the after-party. Still struggling with never-ending problems with cash flow, I looked at my bank balance and thought that I shouldn't go. Then I said, "Screw it," and went anyway. As you will find, I am *really* glad that I did.

I booked a room at the Luxor Hotel, as there were no rooms left at Mandalay Bay, where the show was being held. This was good because the cost of the room at the Luxor was within my credit card limit, and Mandalay Bay was not. I was looking forward not only to the after-party but to getting on a plane and leaving my troubles in Seymour temporarily behind.

Before I left, I called Marc Oswald, Big & Rich's manager, to give him a heads-up that I would be in Vegas and attending the after-party that was going to be held at the House of Blues at Mandalay Bay. Marc was pleased that I was going, yet somewhat mysteriously he told me to bring my wardrobe from the video shoot.

The next few days were a blur and before I knew it I was in the holding tunnel with Big & Rich, dressed in my wardrobe, ready to dance onstage in front of millions of people on national television. I was on the show! It was an amazing experience, and all I could think of was that a few years ago I hadn't been all that into country music, and here I was dancing onstage during the nationally televised Academy of Country Music Awards.

I was on an emotional high during and after the show. I met several of my favorite artists backstage and met even more at the Mafia after-party, including Toby Keith, Kenny Chesney, and Keith Urban, among others.

Later, I sat with Toby Keith until the wee hours of the morning at a bar at Mandalay Bay known to people in the music industry as the Island Bar. Toby was getting ready to go overseas to entertain the troops, and I was struck by his sincere passion for putting smiles on the faces of people who protect our country. As you may know, performing for the troops has not been a onetime event for him. I am so proud to call Toby a friend and fellow American.

This all happened just a month after the video shoot and the entire trip gave me a surreal, cloud-nine feeling, as well as some inkling that there was more in store for me than being a fan who happened to make an appearance in a video. The passing of another four weeks, during which I worked in the real world of real estate, brought me to the CMA Fest and the bus parking area at LP Field.

There I met Gretchen Wilson's then three-and-a-half-year-old daughter, Grace. I've mentioned before that kids are hyperaware of and intrigued by my uniqueness. Grace was no exception. After studying me for a bit, she finally asked, "Why are you so small?"

"Well, Grace, this is the way God made me," I replied.

Gretchen later told me what a perfect answer that was because she, as a parent, didn't have an answer to her daughter's question. In its simplicity, my reply said it all. The rest of that evening Grace and I were best buddies and she often hopped onto my scooter for rides.

Gretchen has been through a lot in her life but it hasn't

affected her ability to be a fantastic mother. She once told me in a conversation about kids, "If it is important to Grace, it is important to me." That statement was extremely powerful and I wish more parents felt that way.

At one point when I was ten the most important thing in life to me was getting a flat tire fixed on my go-kart, but no one around me recognized that. To my parents, the tire was a little thing, but to me it was everything. There is a unique sense of excitement and urgency about things that are important to you when you are a kid, and to not have that importance recognized can be deflating. Gretchen got it then and still gets it.

■   ■   ■

WHILE ATTENDING THE CMA Fest I also attended Big & Rich's last rehearsal before they left to go on tour with Tim McGraw. When I left the rehearsal hall the guys all let me know that I was welcome to come to any show I wanted to and hang out. In my mind this was another opportunity to do something that people rarely experience. When I got back to Seymour I used my dial-up Internet connection to look at Big & Rich's tour schedule. I was extremely pleased and excited to find there were five shows in a row that were all within driving distance of Seymour and each other.

At the first show, at the Riverbend Music Center in Cincinnati, I called the road manager when I got there and he brought me out an all-access laminate. I was floored. This meant I could go anywhere at the venue, including backstage. I watched the show out in the audience and wondered if anyone would recognize me from my brief video appearance. No one that night did.

I went to the next show in Indianapolis, which was wild because I'd been there umpteen times as a fan, but to say I was with the band blew me away. I also went to the show after that in Detroit. Chicago? I was there.

You might wonder how I could run the real estate business and the Funkey Monkey while I was gone so often. The reality is that most of it fell to Toby. I just had a gut feeling that this thing with John Rich and Big Kenny, whatever "it" was, was something that would be important for my future. Throughout my life, when it came to gut feelings, I had grown to trust them, so I was willing to invest a little time and money to see it through.

The last show of that run was on July fourth at Summerfest in Milwaukee. In addition to Big & Rich, who were the middle act on the tour, the show featured Brad and Brett Warren (as the Warren Brothers) as an opening act, with Tim McGraw as the headliner. I specifically remember it was the Fourth of July because Tim's wife, country superstar Faith Hill, was outside their bus setting off sparklers with their girls. I introduced myself, and as a thank-you to Toby for allowing me to take this adventure, I nervously asked if she would leave Toby and Angie a voice mail at the office, and she graciously agreed. It made their day.

Later that night, some of the guys asked me how I was getting to all of the performances, and I told them I was driving to each one. "Well, man, we love having you," they said. Then one of the best things that ever happened to me occurred. John spoke up and said, "For the next show you want to come to, why don't you drive down to Nashville, hop on the bus, and ride with us?"

■ ■ ■

WHILE THE IDEA of riding the bus with the guys was over-the-top exciting, my old friend anxiety bubbled to the surface. The question of how I would use the bathroom, where I'd sit, where my scooter would ride, and a host of other things was in the back of my mind. But none of that discouraged me, and even though I was not yet getting paid I never considered letting this opportunity of a lifetime pass.

My initial impression of life on the bus was one of chaos. First, I learned that the term "bus call" meant departure time and was, to my surprise, at midnight before the following day's show. Loading up before we left, everyone was tossing their bags into a bunk, and they actually had to clear out a space to make room for me. I was the twelfth man on a bus that slept twelve. Oftentimes, buses do not run filled to capacity and leftover bunks are used as junk bunks, catchalls for things that do not fit anywhere else on the bus.

I had never been on a tour bus for any length of time. Certainly I had never been on one that was moving, so I just tried to stay out of everyone's way. I was extremely conscious of not being a hassle to anyone. I feel as if this awareness kept me from being a burden and allowed me to flourish and solidify my position with Big & Rich.

Now I realize that the bus we were on was of middle quality, but back then I was blown away by all the gadgets. Each bunk had its own tiny pull-down television, and there was a larger flat-screen TV in what was called the front lounge. There was also a kitchenette, bathroom, and lots of couch-type seats where we all hung out and talked and drank.

I slept in whatever bottom bunk was open and for the first few nights I didn't sleep well. There was a rocking motion to the bus that took some getting used to. After that, though, I typically passed out rather than fell asleep. That was during a time when alcohol was still a fun thing for me—rather than the cover-up or escape it ultimately became.

At one show I was hanging out in the Warren Brothers' dressing room and they asked if I would introduce them when they came onstage. I said, "Absolutely. Are you kidding me!? Let's do it," and started introducing them to the audience the next night. A few nights later John and Kenny asked why I wasn't doing the same for them. Of course I began introducing them, too. I was excited because now I was not just a guest. I had a "purpose," a reason to stay on the tour, and I needed that to feel validated.

A few nights after I began introducing John and Kenny, they invited me to dance onstage when they performed "Save a Horse (Ride a Cowboy)." I absolutely ate up performing regularly in front of a live audience. It was a rush like no other.

That said, a tour is not all glitz and glamour, as you might think it is. I love what I do, so I'm not complaining, just explaining. There were many places where the physical layout of a building made it difficult for me to take showers, or where I felt dirtier coming out of the shower than I did going in. Canadian hockey arenas, with their lukewarm group locker-room showers, were some of the most "glamorous" arenas we played in.

You are also never alone on a tour. There is always someone around. However, some of those people might or might not be your friend. I met a girl in her early twenties at a multi-artist festival show that we did in the Midwest. I was out in the audience "trolling for girls," spotted her, and asked if she wanted to come backstage. She got on my scooter and I took her to where everyone was hanging out. We had cocktails and hung out again after the show.

We had a lot of shows in her area that summer and I saw her several times. The second time I saw her we made out. Then we began flirting over the phone. Or so I thought. I thought we had the beginnings of a relationship. Several months went by where we spoke on the phone several times a week.

One day she was with a group of friends when she left me what started out to be a sweet voice mail. "Fred, I can't wait to see you. I hope all is well. Love you, bye." Then she thought she had disconnected the call, but she hadn't. The next thing I heard was the girl saying to her friends, "That was the midget I used to get backstage at the Big & Rich shows." It was also very obvious that she was quite proud of the fact that she used me. The voice mail went on for four long minutes until it cut off.

I was in shock when I first heard the message. Then my shock turned to grief, then to anger, and then, sadly, to deep skepticism of every new person I met. The message was crushing to me and furthered my inability to trust. Still, I have many true friends whom I met on the road that I know are not like that, but I did meet several more who were. Early on I was very naïve to the ways of some people. I come from a background of strong, hard-working, trustworthy, and honest people and it was hard for me to realize that not everyone is this way.

■ ■ ■

I BEGAN DANCING to "Save a Horse (Ride a Cowboy)" as a regular part of the show. Then Roberts Brothers Coaches, the company Big & Rich leased their bus from, made me a "throne" at the request of John and Kenny. The throne offered me an opportunity to sit down and rest between dancing instead of sitting on the stage where no one could see me. I used that throne for several years and after it was no longer part of the stage layout, ironically, it went on display as a museum piece . . . at Fontanel of all places. I think back to waking up on the couch in the great room at Fontanel and continue to be amazed at how things circle around.

At each show I participated more and more, and fans began to recognize me. Slowly but surely, Two Foot Fred was becoming something of a country music icon.

16

ALWAYS PUSHING
THE LIMITS

About a month before we shot the "Save a Horse (Ride a Cowboy)" video, John sent me an e-mail that asked if it was okay if they "lovingly" referred to me as Two Foot Fred on the set. It was a name John came up with and I, of course, said absolutely. Even though I am three feet two inches tall, I do not think John knew that at the time. Besides, I think the name has a nice ring to it. "Three Foot Fred" just doesn't roll off your tongue as well. Besides, I have a lot of fun explaining my name.

Also during shows on tour the Bud Light rep George Ewasko took out a bottle for Tim McGraw to drink during the song "I Like It, I Love It." Bud Light was the sponsor of Tim's tour, and it was the perfect point in the show to give them a plug. After I got to know George, he began letting me be the one to take out not only Tim's Bud Light, but also one for myself to throw back with Tim onstage. How cool is that?

Since then, I have learned that not many headliners would have been as humble and generous as Tim McGraw was in promoting both Cowboy Troy and me. Cowboy Troy is a tall, black country rap artist who was also part of the MuzikMafia. He is an amazing human being and someone you should get to know, if you ever have the chance. Over the years he has become one of my best friends.

Troy was fresh out of being an assistant manager at Foot Locker in Dallas, Texas. Due to John Rich's innate skill at plugging in talented friends, Troy was on the tour with us. During Tim's performance of "She's My Kind of Rain," he invited Troy to come out onstage with him and rap in the middle of the song. It was something that could have been quite controversial back then but turned out to be a crowd favorite. It speaks highly of Tim's instinct as one of our industry's leading performers. If Tim had not been so secure as an artist, and as a person, that never would have happened.

I loved being onstage and at first I wore whatever I had on, but after several shows, and thinking this might turn into a real situation, I quickly realized that I had to dress the part. I decided to jazz up my onstage presence with a big, red and orange striped fuzzy top hat that I had from an old Halloween costume. To that I added a long, red feather boa and a red, orange, and yellow tie-dyed Funkey Monkey T-shirt. Mom helped out by dying a pair of my khakis bright red. As you can see, my onstage wardrobe was an evolving process. It came together piece by piece and the result was that I looked like a pimp on Halloween. Because my position with Big & Rich was so organic, so was my outfit. It all happened so slowly that at first I didn't even think I needed to dress for the stage.

When I was on my throne, I was quite the fun-loving cartoon character. In the beginning many people questioned whether I was being exploited in a negative way. My response is and always has been: "First of all, the word 'exploit' can refer to both positive and negative situations." I also reminded them that the real question should be, "Just who is exploiting whom?" I was having a blast and if it wasn't for John Rich I would not have had this opportunity. Most people's perception is that to exploit, someone has to take unfair advantage of another for his or her personal gain. This opportunity was in no way unfair, no one was being taken advantage of, and I was the one who was benefiting from it. If this was exploitation, then bring it on.

I do realize that part of the attraction is my size, but I look at my new career in entertainment as an opportunity to educate people about others who have physical differences, as a way to "exploit" my creativity, meet some great people, and also, quite frankly, have a lot of fun.

Later, around 2006, John had enough foresight to realize that I couldn't dress like a cartoon character forever, so I switched to a rock and roll T-shirt, jeans, and a custom vest topped with a fedora hat. I wore the pimp outfit for several years.

■ ■ ■

AS THE SUMMER of 2004 progressed, my thirtieth birthday was looming. I had always wanted to do something special to celebrate this milestone, but never in a million years did I ever think I would spend it on ABC's *Jimmy Kimmel Live!*

A few years earlier, Jimmy Kimmel had been part of the NFL's football coverage. During one segment they did a lighthearted spoof that featured dwarves who impersonated sports commentators. After the segment ran, the female co-host said something to the effect of, "Wasn't that great?" to which Jimmy commented something like, "Yeah, midgets are fun. Everyone should own one." That comment incensed me. The word "midget" to a little person is an offensive label because it is associated with circus acts and sideshows from the early 1900s, when "midgets" were paid attractions.

When I mentioned it to John he said, "Good, we are going to do Jimmy's show and you are going to be on it." On the show I wore a T-shirt that said, "Jimmy Kimmel can kiss my dwarf ass." When Jimmy asked me what the T-shirt was about all I said was, "It's karma, Jimmy. Karma."

Jimmy was very cool after the show and hung out with us. I am sure that Jules Wortman, the publicist for Warner Bros. Records, had set the entire thing up. There was no way either Big & Rich or the record label would ambush Jimmy's show like that. Jules was also responsible for getting me included in a lot of Big & Rich television appearances. Thank you, Jules!

After the show, John and Kenny took us all out to celebrate at a restaurant called Ago that was owned by Robert De Niro. You have to realize that at this point in their career, in the middle of their first tour, John and Kenny did not have a lot of money. They were still struggling, as were the rest of us. That evening we ran up a three-thousand-dollar wine bill and John and Kenny covered the entire thing. At the time, while I was appreciative of that generous gesture I did not fully appreciate the magnitude of what had just happened. I am so grateful that they went to so much trouble to make my first birthday away from home so special.

To make it even better, the drummer's friend Corrine and her mom got me a cake. That gesture was so thoughtful and appreciated. Sometimes it is the little things that make life complete. The cake was unexpected but something I really needed. I regret to say that our drummer and friend Brian Barnett has since passed away. He was a fantastic drummer so he's probably playing drums for Johnny Cash or Hank Williams Sr. in heaven.

My birthday celebration wasn't the only thing that made that trip memorable. At that time on the road we kept my scooter in a merchandise trailer that was pulled behind the bus. The day before, at a show in Sacramento, I had been riding around backstage with a girl on my scooter, which was often the case. However, this time, even though I knew I had jumped a curb, I didn't realize there was anything wrong. However, when they unloaded my scooter for *Jimmy Kimmel Live!* the next day, I was shocked to find it was in two pieces. The frame had snapped. Although it created a feeling of helplessness, I am never one to be deterred. I had one of the crew lift me onto a road case, and they rolled me into the building in fine fashion on top of it.

The next day, in Albuquerque, we found that one of the venue's local stagehands used to be a race car builder. He noticed some of our crew inspecting my scooter to see what could be done to fix it and jumped into action. This venue also had an extensive workshop, which is not the case for most amphitheaters. To this day I believe the availability of the workshop and the skill of the stagehand (along with our front-of-house engineer Martin Frey, our production manager Curt Jenkins, and our set carpenter Mike "Moses" Beck) in fixing my scooter was definitely not a coincidence. These guys took the scooter completely apart and put it back together again in perfect working order. I wish I could remember the name of the gentleman from the venue who made the rest of the trip easier for me. In hopes that he is reading this book, I can't thank him enough.

■ ■ ■

AS THE MONTHS passed, I'd go out with the tour for a week or so and then go back to Seymour to deal with the growing mound of problems our real estate business was going through: from plumbing troubles in occupied units, to refurbishing empty apartments, to a never-ending turnover of tenants.

By this time, even though my goal had been to own five hundred units, we were more than consumed time-wise with two hundred fifty-nine. Although I would never have admitted it then, it was more than we could handle, even if I had been there all the time. Plus, my transition from real estate to entertainment happened so slowly and organically that I truly felt I could handle both careers. But as time passed, even though I still would not admit it, I could see the business was suffering.

Probably at this juncture the right thing to do would have been to jump back. Most people would have seen there was too much going on and, out of fear, backed away from one career or the other. But me being me, I chose to deal with the situation by diving even farther into my role as an entertainer. Being on the road opened up a whole new world for me. For the first time in many years I felt validated. The restaurant and real estate businesses had knocked me off my feet, but the thrill and perks of the road invigorated me.

One of those perks included the ladies. I had a pretty good time meeting a lot of them after our shows. Our bass player and I went what we called "trolling" during McGraw's set. We were like kids in a candy store, often inviting more than one girl to come back and hang with the band. I didn't date anyone regularly, and in fact, I never have. It made it that much sweeter that there never was a shortage of girls around. Besides living in the moment, which sometimes meant making out and drinking, several of the girls I met at various venues have become friends, and I enjoy staying in touch with them through Facebook.

■   ■   ■

BY NOW I not only was part of the regular show, I had a title. I was named the official Ambassador of Attractions for Big & Rich. I can't tell you how excited this made me. I was becoming thoroughly engrossed in this new world and loved every second of it.

As I mentioned, until this point I was doing all of this on my own, which means I was not getting paid. Actually, I probably would have paid them to have these experiences! The subject came up during the 2005 tour with Brooks & Dunn, but John and Kenny were still not at a place financially where they could justify paying me. I then asked if I could sell one item at the merchandise booth to help pay for the gas I was spending to drive back and forth between Seymour and Nashville. Management reasoned that because of the large number of items already available in the merch booth, my request had to be denied. John then, off the record, suggested I mention my dilemma to Kix Brooks in hopes that he could overturn this decision he didn't know about in the first place.

Lo and behold the perfect time arose for me to broach the subject with Kix. This was a Coors Light–sponsored tour and after Kix and I spent some time supporting our sponsor we found ourselves chatting on his bus.

I asked Kix, "May I ask you a question, sir?"

"Absolutely," he said. "What's on your mind?"

I told him that I wasn't being paid for my duties as Two Foot Fred. "Don't get me wrong," I assured him. "I love doing it and I'm not asking you for money."

"You mean John and Kenny aren't paying your little ass?" he asked with a smile.

"No," I said, "but that's okay because I want to do it."

Kix then asked what he could do. I mentioned that I'd like to be able to sell one T-shirt on the road. Not wanting to throw anyone under the bus, I only said that management had discussed it and said no.

"We'll take care of that," Kix said, "but there is one condition. I get the first shirt."

Right away I got some shirts made and began to sell around thirty shirts a night, which more than covered my expenses and made me extremely happy. Having a merch item also made me feel more secure—like an official entertainer.

The shirts were a bright orange tie-dye with a picture of me in an orange hat and sunglasses with my hands raised. The name of the tour was the "Deuces Wild" tour because there were three duos: the Warren Brothers, Big & Rich, and Brooks & Dunn. On the back of the shirt was "The Deuce is wild." That how I got my other nickname, "the Deuce."

■ ■ ■

I HAD ALSO been spending more and more time in Nashville. Up to now, when I was in Music City I had been staying with a friend I'd met at a MuzikMafia event in New York, Carolyn Miller. Carolyn worked in the artist management side of Nashville's music business and had a futon in her extra bedroom that I often, and thankfully, slept on.

Carolyn lived in an apartment complex off Hillsboro Road very close to Music Row. I knew that if I was going to continue to tour with Big & Rich, eventually I'd have to have my own space in Nashville—for her sake and mine. So Carolyn introduced me to her apartment manager, Mrs. Rucker. Mrs. Rucker had managed the apartment complex for more than forty years. Her daughter had been one of the previous Mrs. Harlan Howards (Harlan Howard was a famous songwriter) and Mrs. Rucker had a lot of stories she'd go on and on about. It also appeared that Mrs. Rucker was a bit lonely and enjoyed my company as she'd talk my ear off before I could tell her what was on my mind.

After enduring a few of these "chat sessions" I was happy to hear that a ground-floor apartment that was perfect for me had become available. I promptly paid the deposit and made plans to move. My plan was to live in Seymour full-time and only be in Nashville when I was needed, but that soon changed to living in Nashville full-time and being in Seymour when I was needed. It took me four years, but I finally sold my house in Seymour. The first two years I didn't even have the house on the market out of a fear of commitment, and the last two years it was on the market but didn't sell due to the real estate crash. So for four years I sacrificed to pay both mortgage and rent, just so I could do what I loved. I finally sold the house for much less than I paid for it.

I was not well-off financially. Really, at this point I was scraping by on credit cards to make things work. I had learned my lesson about gambling, but it took me years to pay off the credit cards.

On January 2, 2006, the maintenance guys from our real estate company helped me move into my new home, my apartment in Nashville. I couldn't have been more excited.

■ ■ ■

A WONDERFUL OPPORTUNITY for national exposure came about for me not too long after I got my apartment in Nashville. Cowboy Troy had been selected to host the USA network's country music reality show, *Nashville Star*. *Nashville Star* was an *American Idol*–style show with country artists. Through my connection with Big & Rich's management, and with Cowboy Troy, I was added to do the exit interviews. My job was to interview the latest contestant to be eliminated from the competition while the credits rolled. The interviews were always filled with emotion, because the person I was interviewing had just gotten their hopes and dreams squashed.

I took this opportunity very seriously and must have done a good job because I was hired back for a second year. My catch-phrase for the show was "It's time for you to hit the bricks." I know that while it was not mainstream a lot of country fans watched the show, because people say the phrase to me all the time.

Being part of *Nashville Star* was a great experience, but I had to get back on tour with Big & Rich and was beyond pumped that one of the places we were performing was the Funkey Monkey during Oktoberfest.

I had been watching for a date where we'd be going north on I-65 from Nashville with a day off before the show. That off day was important because I knew with the right approach I could get the guys to play in Seymour. The perfect date appeared when we were to play Indianapolis with the Brooks & Dunn tour and had that coveted day before off. Most performance contracts have a clause that states that an artist cannot perform within a certain geographical radius of another performance within a certain time period, usually at least thirty days and ninety miles. Because of that clause, we could not advertise the show, as it was too close to the show in Indianapolis, but the guys agreed to perform anyway. Just by word of mouth it sold out.

I was wound up about bringing all of my new friends to my hometown and to my own bar. The show did really well, even with a high-dollar ticket price, and everyone had a great time. In fact, the concert and after-party turned into a free-for-all. It was one of those nights when everything went right. After the show John and Kenny tended bar for a while before the band, crew, and I got on the bus to head out for Indianapolis.

Every artist cherishes the opportunity to play in his or her hometown, and I was no different. I knew everyone around, but this was the first time anyone other than my family had seen me in my new role. I really wanted it to be a total success, and it was!

In the minds of people from my hometown, the fact that Big & Rich performed at our little bar went a long way toward quieting the nonsense that circulated in Seymour about my new career. As Big & Rich's career began to grow, and after my first season on *Nashville Star*, I began to notice subtle changes in how I was treated at home. When I visited my hometown, people would say one of two things, either "I'm really happy for your success" or "Wow, you're not too big to come back to little Seymour." I know my newfound success also created some envy but I didn't let it bother me. Mostly, I am humbled and honored when people tell me they are happy for my success.

Other than that, however, life went on pretty much as before when I was home, mainly because Seymour has had more than its share of celebrity. Rock icon John Cougar Mellencamp is from Seymour, as is Olympic swimmer Pat Calhoun. I have already mentioned wrestler Rip Rogers, and Mark Emkes, older brother of fellow Seymour dwarf Jana Emkes, became the CEO of tire giant Bridgestone Americas. In 2009, Seymour native Katie Stam would be crowned Miss America.

We are from different generations, but we all represent Seymour. Today when I visit my hometown, people are mostly inquisitive and supportive. They want to know where to go when they visit Nashville, who my favorite celebrities are, and what's next for me. It is now a friendly conversation, rather than envious, as it once was.

■ ■ ■

WITH MY INCREASING profile I was now gaining my own fan base. I found it amazing that people not only stood in line for my autograph at shows, some even began driving from show to show to see me, just as I had once done to see Big & Rich. Another circle completed.

What was interesting was that most people understood what I was doing in the entertainment business. Most people, that is, except my parents. At least, this was the case until I invited them to a show we did with Tim McGraw in Dayton, Ohio, which was as close to Seymour as we would be. After the performance, after my parents saw me onstage, I took them back to meet Tim and Faith. My parents had a fantastic time and finally *got it*.

That said, to my dad I was still "his Fred" and he did not understand the scope of Two Foot Fred. In July of 2008, I took Dad, Toby, and a friend to the Brickyard 400 NASCAR race. Because of my friendship with driver Ryan Newman, whom I'd met through my country music connections, I had an all-access season pass and was able to get them all-access day passes. While I was showing them around the garage area, a fan of mine came up and wanted his picture taken with me. Of course I agreed.

As we were walking away Dad asked me if I knew "that guy," and I said, "No, why?" Then Dad asked why, if I didn't know the person, he would want a photo of us together.

I said, "Dad, I'm Two Foot Fred," to which he replied, "Oh . . . oh, yeah . . ." I think Dad had a lightbulb moment there. In the meantime Toby was laughing so hard at the incident that I thought he was going to fall off his scooter.

In another mind-blowing fan situation, Mrs. Downing, my first-grade teacher, came through my autograph line one year at the convention center at the CMA Music Festival. It was interesting because she used to help me to the bathroom, and now she was asking for my autograph. I loved seeing her and being able to say hi.

As Ambassador of Attractions I also began doing media interviews and promotions: radio, television, print, and Internet. I know a lot of artists and celebrities abhor doing media, but I love it. I get to meet a lot of great people and have a ton of fun in the process. What could be better than that? Well, there are a few things.

Even though a fair amount of interviews are done by phone, I sometimes get to meet the personalities who interview me at events like CRS (the Country Radio Seminar, which is held in Nashville every spring); the CMA Music Fest; or the CMA, ACM, or CMT awards. Meeting people face-to-face is a blast, because I am able to learn more about them and their circumstances.

This is important because I have a unique talent for connecting people who otherwise may never have met. Because I know so many people, I have been able to connect media reps with businessmen, athletes with entertainers, businessmen with athletes and entertainers—it goes on and on. Along the way I create lasting relationships with all of the parties involved. In many ways people have said I am the consummate dot connector.

But all was not rosy in my world. In 2006 the United States entered the beginning stages of what would be a national real estate crisis. With a company that was already on the edge, what was happening in the economy was the proverbial nail in the coffin. While my parents and I continually butted heads about our exit strategy, we started selling off some of our apartment units, but our timing was too late.

Small towns are the first to feel the pinch of a recession. After the first hint of national economic troubles hit, it was tough to sell anything, let alone sell apartments for what we owed on them, much less for a profit. Some we sold at a loss, some we let the bank have back, some we hung on to. A new kind of hell was on the horizon for Toby and me, and its name was Chapter 11 bankruptcy.

RECHARGING
BY GIVING BACK

Around the time of the Republican conven-
tion in 2008, Big & Rich, Cowboy Troy, and I began to travel with
Republican presidential candidate John McCain. I cannot state
what a supreme honor and a privilege this was. But before I tell
you about that, I have to go back to my political roots.

My dad first ran for office, unsuccessfully, for Jackson County
councilman in 1976. The first election I remember was in 1980,
when he ran a successful campaign for county commissioner.
I remember being at our local Republican headquarters waiting anxiously for election results. Then, when we knew Dad was
going to win, Toby and I were dropped off at Aunt Linda's while
Mom and Dad celebrated at the county courthouse in Brownstown.

Dad ran again in 1984, when I was ten, and this time I was
old enough to be taken out of school to help Dad campaign on

Election Day. Because my teachers saw this as a learning experience they were supportive of my absence. I loved being with Dad and I thought it was cool that so many people knew and respected him.

Four years later, in 1988, another election rolled around. At fourteen, my friends and I had enough maturity that we could campaign for Dad at the polls on our own. We started our day at six A.M. and worked hard. At lunch we were ready to eat when Mom brought us food from McDonald's. Our campaigning worked, because Dad was elected then, and several more times.

I didn't realize it at the time, but these elections and campaigns taught me a lot about the political process and about how the business side of our government works—at least on a local level. By 1992 Toby and I were riding our scooters in local parades and handing out campaign pins and materials. But that year Dad lost by a small margin, and for the first time my family and I had a personal experience with political defeat. Dad truly felt he had been making a difference in our county and in people's lives, and wanted to continue doing so. One of the things I admire about him is that for the next four years he kept getting out and talking to people to find out what was important to them. I have to state that Dad didn't do this out of political aspiration, as most of the candidates did; he did it because he cared.

Throughout these four years, and his entire political career, we as a family attended a lot of church dinners. Sometimes it seems as if I grew up on turkey and dumplings, and chicken and noodle dinners, along with some pretty decent homemade desserts.

In 1996 Dad won his seat back and kept it until 2008, so

twenty-four out of twenty-eight years, Dad gave back to his community in a big way. Dad may not have been around much when Toby and I were small, but I am very proud of his service to Seymour, and to Jackson County.

All of this background ensured that when I turned eighteen, I began to vote. I am proud of the fact that I have voted in every election I was eligible to vote in. Voting is one privilege that we enjoy in our country that too many people either take for granted or do not utilize. We as citizens of the United States have choices. We have a vote. We can change the direction of our country, but to do that we have to get out to the polls on Election Day. I personally know that every vote counts because one year Dad won by a seven-vote margin. Also, I believe my early campaigning was the foundation for my dot connecting.

In 2008, when it was fairly certain that Arizona senator John McCain was going to be the Republican nominee, John Rich wrote a song and self-funded a music video called "Raising McCain." The song quickly came to the attention of the McCain campaign and before any of us realized it, John, Cowboy Troy, and I were stumping on the campaign trail.

We appeared at a few campaign events and rallies locally in Tennessee. Then, the week of the Republican convention, we had a tour date in Oklahoma, after which we flew to Pittsburgh to take part in a national rally. This was the day after Sarah Palin was announced as the vice presidential candidate, so you can imagine the huge buzz going on around the campaign. The energy and busy-ness of the campaign was unbelievable.

At the Pittsburgh rally, John performed "Raising McCain," along with a couple of other patriotic songs, and then both

McCain and Palin spoke to a sold-out crowd—and to several standing ovations.

After the rally we all boarded campaign buses. John was on the McCain bus and I ended up on the press bus with the rest of our group. Next thing I know we are in the middle of, and part of, a presidential candidate's motorcade. Freeways and exit ramps were closed so our travels would be quick and safe. It was quite the bizarre experience! The motorcade stopped at the airport, where we boarded the Straight Talk Express, a private 747 used by the McCain campaign. I was ecstatic when our group was invited to sit up front with the McCain family. The press and campaign staffers were relegated to the back of the plane, and while I was happy to be there in any capacity, it was a real honor to sit up front.

We were already seated when Sarah Palin boarded with her husband, Todd, and daughters Bristol and Piper. For those of you who have not met Sarah, she has incredible charisma. She is also a huge, huge, *huge* fan of Big & Rich. She and her sister's all-time favorite song is "Save a Horse (Ride a Cowboy)," or so she told John that day. Piper was so smitten with John Rich that she practically sat in his lap the entire flight.

I ended up sitting across the aisle from Senator McCain's daughter Meghan, and in the space of just a few minutes, we bonded. She was very inquisitive about my size and me. I love it when people ask questions because it allows me the opportunity to educate people about dwarfism, and also to have them understand I am just like them, only shorter.

By the time we got to the hotel at our next rally in St. Louis, Meghan and I were new best friends. Later that evening she and most of the campaign staffers and I hung out in the hotel restaurant, where we all got to know each other a little better.

The next morning I found out that being part of a national presidential campaign is interesting, to say the least. Exactly one hour before you were to leave the hotel, your bags had to be packed and out in the hallway for the Secret Service guys to pick up, scan, and leave for you to collect from a holding room. Plus, anytime a presidential candidate is moving around the hotel, everyone is on lockdown. I mean absolutely everyone. For example, we were finishing breakfast when Senator McCain returned from his quick trip to the Gulf Coast after Hurricane Gustav and we had to stay put until the senator was in his room.

Another thing I learned was that the family and key campaign people had lapel pins that designated their level of access. And the family pins had chips in them that were monitored by the Secret Service.

That day we flew to Minneapolis, where the senator later joined us. Because Senator McCain had the big plane for another rally, we all flew on a smaller plane that Cindy McCain often used.

On that flight, Meghan McCain gave her pin to me. It was no secret that she loathed the Secret Service. But after what was probably a long, confusing day for them, the Secret Service guys figured it out and I was respectfully asked to give the pin back to Meghan, which, of course, I did. I later found out that what we did, while it was all in fun, was incompliant with federal law.

This was another exciting plane ride for me because several other notable people were on board, including Mitt Romney and Mike Huckabee, along with the Palins.

With Meghan were two of her friends that she called the

"Blogettes." Shannon was the videographer and Heather was the photographer. They blogged daily about the campaign and campaign life. Several of the blogs spoke of our group and the fresh energy and morale boost that was created with our participation. It was a lot of fun, especially when we finally arrived at the Republican National Convention.

As a lifelong Republican, I was excited about attending my first Republican (RNC) national convention, and the reality of that was above and beyond my wildest expectations. I was more than awestruck, especially when I learned that we would be watching the event from the Palin family box. I made many new friends, including Todd Palin's brother J.D., whom I still e-mail with regularly.

One of the highlights of my trip was having my photo taken with former United States secretary of state Henry Kissinger. He is such an admirable man that it was great to meet him in person.

On a different note, I was a bit alarmed to realize exactly how much restraint candidates at a national level are under. A presidential candidate is surrounded by Secret Service—and others—who not only watch out for a candidate's safety, they intercept the candidate's interactions with the media, family and friends, and the general public. I do understand the need for this from a safety standpoint. However, I thought it was to a level that was almost sickening. Senator McCain had absolutely no freedom and no hope of privacy throughout the campaign.

After my experience, my hope is that future candidates will be allowed to be more genuine and not be afraid that every little move will be so overanalyzed and deconstructed by the media that the original meaning and intent is lost. With our current twenty-four-hour news channels, often the talking heads do not have enough to talk about. Then abstract thinking—and off-the-cuff remarks about a candidate—can be considered by the viewer as fact. It can all quickly get out of hand.

I do hope for my country's sake, for the sake of my children, grandchildren, and great-grandchildren, that we never again have a *political change* such as we had in 2008. Throughout the campaign, our participation was on a completely volunteer basis, and I loved the fact that John Rich allowed me to help him contribute to the political process. For someone like me to go from local elections in Jackson County, Indiana, as an elementary school kid in the early 1980s to being part of a presidential campaign in 2008, again, the circle remains unbroken.

■   ■   ■

IN ADDITION TO being able to influence our country's direction by lending my support to the political process, I also enjoyed helping the many charitable causes that were beginning to come my way. I especially loved using my status as a platform for public education about people in need from different walks of life. I wanted to show the world that not only is there nothing a dwarf cannot do, but there is nothing anyone can't do.

Once again I set goals and challenges for myself, but this was the first time any of my goals would positively impact people other than just myself. This time, I had the opportunity to give hope to millions of people who are impacted daily by disabilities and life in general. And while I wasn't yet anywhere close to where I needed to be (and knew I eventually would be), I found there was a spiritual aspect to giving back. The more you give, the more you get. Plus, I realized that no matter how bad life could be at times for me, there was always someone else who had it worse; there was always someone I could help.

In 2007 Big & Rich and I co-hosted the first annual ACM Charity Poker Tournament that was held at the MGM Grand Hotel and Casino in Las Vegas. Proceeds went to the ACM charitable fund, which helps a number of worthy causes. Photos of me from that tournament have shown up all over the place and further my goal of empowering people with disabilities to live full and active lives.

That same year I also participated in the ACM Charity Motorcycle Ride, which also benefits the ACM foundation. And I was happy to help my friend Ryan Newman with his Ryan Newman Foundation Charity Gala & Auction. This event enriches the lives of people and animals throughout our nation. As you will see in the next chapter, I love animals and know they provide unconditional love. They also have an amazing healing power. Ryan's foundation was definitely a cause I could, and do, support.

From the annual City of Hope Celebrity Softball Challenge, which raises money for City of Hope, a leading research, education, and treatment center for cancer and other life-threatening diseases, to events for St. Jude Children's Research Hospital and beyond, I am honored to contribute to these worthy causes.

I am also excited about founding my own charity, the Freddie Foundation, to foster the human privilege of mobility through education and charitable collection of funds to be spent on the overall mobility needs of the less fortunate. Especially when it comes to children. You might think this is readily provided through insurance and government programs, but that is not always the case. I feel a calling to create awareness of this effort and know the foundation will be a huge success in doing so. I had actually begun working on founding my charity when a blow far greater than anything I had yet experienced in life derailed me.

18

UNCOVERING AND HOLDING ON TO IMPORTANT VALUES

We are all a product of our upbringing, and I am no exception. Many of the values my parents and grandparents instilled in me at a young age are still with me. But as you have seen, while I had great parents, I did not have perfect parents. No one does. I love my mom and dad wholeheartedly, but we still had our unique set of issues and individual ways of doing things.

Over the past few years I realized I have harbored some resentment toward my mom due to her enabling. I have since worked through that and continue to realize she was the best mother she could be.

With all that said, it was a complete shock to find out on January 30, 2008, that Mom had lung cancer. It shouldn't have been such a surprise because Mom had smoked since the age of fifteen, which was more than fifty years. Until a parent becomes critically ill, I believe every child, even adult children, has it in their mind that their parent is invincible. I'm sorry to say, that's not true.

A few days before Mom was officially diagnosed with small-cell carcinoma, she had gone to the hospital after feeling extremely fatigued and ill. A that time it was discovered she had a severe deficiency in her sodium levels. Mom had always been a little bit of a hypochondriac, so when I was first told the news I didn't think too much about it, other than I hoped she would get well soon.

The night she was admitted to the hospital I was out on the town in Nashville when I received a text from Toby. He suggested I call Mom immediately. When I heard the fear in her voice, in hindsight, I think she already suspected it was something far worse than a sodium deficiency. The hospital ran more tests and a lung cancer diagnosis was confirmed.

I wish I could say I felt the pain of Mom's diagnosis deeply. The truth was, at the time, I was emotionally numb to her situation. Some people might call it denial, and that may very well be what it was. So much had happened to me over the past ten years: the rise and fall of my dreams for Fred N' Toby's; the birth and struggle of the real estate business; my drinking, partying, and gambling; my obsession with women; the high of discovering joy in a new career in entertainment. And now this. There is only so much a person can handle before becoming overwhelmed.

In my case, I shifted to the next gear, which was a combination of numbness and taking control. So instead of being emotionally supportive I began researching every possible treatment scenario I could find. That was all I knew to do. Get information.

Find help. Discover a way to make the cancer go away. Again, I was trying to fix something that was out of my control.

Both Toby and I encouraged Mom to get second and even third opinions, so she and Dad headed to the renowned Mayo Clinic in Rochester, Minnesota. Mom only went after a lot of pushing on our part. Dad later confided to Toby and me that when Mom was there, she found a broken cigarette in her purse. While he was running an errand she taped it back together and smoked it. That's how strong of a hold cigarettes had on her.

The results from Mom's visit to Mayo were in line with her first diagnosis from our local oncologist. Dad seemed to have his head in the sand about the entire situation. I now know we each deal with stress and tragedy in our lives in different ways. Dad's was to do what he knew best, and that was to work. Maybe he thought if he stayed busy enough that it would keep his mind off of Mom's having cancer.

I continued my fact-finding mission and tapped into some of my celebrity connections. One day I had a very productive half-hour phone conversation with former Olympic gold medalist skater Scott Hamilton. He graciously offered to make a referral for us at the Cleveland Clinic, where he had been cured of testicular cancer a few years back. I thanked him for the offer and told him we'd be in touch if that was the direction we decided to go in.

I spent that summer worrying quite a bit about Mom and praying that the round of chemo that had been prescribed would work. The research I had done made me aware there was only a 5 percent chance of her surviving this ordeal. But 5 percent does not mean impossible.

This was the same summer as the Republican National Convention and our campaigning with Senator McCain. I was also out on tour with Big & Rich and involved in several charity events. There was a lot going on, and I was not in Seymour nearly as much as I would have liked.

■ ■ ■

DURING THIS TIME Mom had two dogs that kept her company. Jenny and Susie became an important part of her daily living, and ultimately, her dying process. I believe God placed animals here on Earth to help us, and Jenny and Susie certainly did that for Mom.

Susie was originally my dog. I got her around 2000 when I was pursuing a girl whose dog had a litter of chow-mix puppies. The relationship with the girl never panned out but Susie remained an important part of our family. I was living with Mom and Dad then and came home one day and said, "Mom, I want you to meet Susie."

Mom, of course, said, "What is that?"

I said, "What do you think it is? It's a puppy."

Mom asked whose puppy it was, and when I told her it was ours she jumped into a speech about not wanting to take care of a dog. Long story short, two days later you could not have pried Mom and Susie apart. They adored each other. Dad was soon to follow.

The addition of Susie to our family brought up reminders of the dog Toby and I had when we were kids. When I was about five, my parents took me into the country to see a litter of beagle hound puppies. They had a white-and-fawn-colored female that I liked, but she was spoken for, so we chose a black, brown, and white male that I promptly named Scooby. This was during the time when I was a *Scooby-Doo* fanatic.

While he was a puppy, Scooby lived in a crate in the garage. I played with him before and after school, but as he grew larger, Scooby began knocking us over and was chained to a doghouse in our backyard. This was twenty-five years ago when chaining a dog up in a yard was not considered a bad thing to do. Now I look back and regret that deeply. However, I was young and didn't know any different, not that I would have had any say in the matter anyway.

As the years passed, Scooby began to jump on us, so our interactions decreased. Then he began to bark. Poor Scooby was probably desperate for attention but the noise was causing problems with our neighbors so Dad took Scooby out to the farm near our cabin. Dad was in and out of the farm regularly, so he took care of him. One day Dad went over there to find Scooby had disappeared, and we never saw him again. I have a feeling someone shot him, but I desperately hope I am wrong. I feel terrible that while Scooby was never mistreated, he also was never loved. Everyone, everything, deserves to be loved.

After that, Toby and I had rabbits: Brownie, Blacky, and Wilma (who ended up being a boy), along with several others. Once the process started it was like pouring water on Gizmo from the movie *Gremlins*. We had rabbits coming out of our ears and they kept Toby and me entertained for a long time. We played with them in the house, and Dad also built a rabbit cage with steps on the outside so Toby and I could interact with them better. I can truly say those rabbits were loved.

As a family, we bestowed all the love we had never given Scooby on Susie. She became an inside-outside dog who had the run of the house and the yard, and as she matured, she became quite protective of our family. A few years later, when I bought the house that Toby and I lived in across the block from Mom and Dad's, we knew Susie's unsociable personality would not mesh with our friends wandering in and out of the house. Susie was a one-family dog, so she unofficially became Mom and Dad's, rather than mine.

Jenny was added to our family after she was featured as "Dog of the Day" in the Seymour *Tribune*. I saw Jenny's picture and was compelled to go to the Jackson County Humane Society to inquire about adopting her. When I went into the pen where she was housed, Jenny clung to my side. I knew right away that she was my dog. She was a sweet springer spaniel/border collie mix who was about six months old.

I learned shortly after taking Jenny home that she had been scheduled to be euthanized several days before but, because she was such a sweetheart, the staff could not do it. Jenny was about half the size of Susie. Although she lived with Toby and me, we often took her to see Susie. When Toby moved out I kept Jenny until Mom began taking her home with her when I was on the road. Mom and Dad ended up unofficially keeping Jenny at their house.

■ ■ ■

AS 2008 WORE on, the continued chemo treatments wore Mom down. The few times I went home I saw significant changes in Mom's physical condition. Although she was very proud of the wig she picked out when chemo made her lose all of her hair, seeing her was beyond heartbreaking. I don't think Toby and Dad were as aware of it because they saw Mom on a daily basis.

As my research had predicted, Mom's first round of chemotherapy cleared her body of the cancer—for the time being. To be officially cancer free there has to be a five-year period of remission and we were taking it week by week. After four weeks of not having cancer we received the news that it had returned, this time in droves. It not only attacked her lungs but spread to her liver.

Mom was placed back on chemo and received radiation treatments on her brain in an attempt to prevent the cancer from spreading there. My research also told me this was common practice. Even though Mom and Dad questioned the effectiveness of the radiation they agreed to have the process done. The preventative radiation worked; however, the cancer was resistant to the second series of chemo and was running rampant. By that time, her weeks were numbered.

In late October, I received a call from Toby, who told me that Dad had taken Mom to the hospital and I should head to Seymour as soon as I could, which I did. I knew deep down Mom would probably never leave the hospital. She should have been in hospice long before this, but for whatever reason, she wasn't.

Mom couldn't smoke in the hospital and she missed the act of smoking to the point of grieving. All the addictive things cigarette manufacturers put in their cigarettes should be illegal. I wish just one of them could sit and watch one of their "customers" die. Maybe it would change their mind about what they are doing to the people of our country and around the world. Then again, maybe not.

In the hospital the three of us, Toby, Dad, and I, sat at Mom's bedside. Aunt Linda and the girls were also a steady presence. Grandma Gill visited, as did various members of our extended family. Toby and I took breaks, but I think reality had finally arrived for Dad and he did not want to leave. After about three days Toby and I made Dad go home so he could shower and change clothes.

At her bedside, Mom and the rest of us had two or three days of off-and-on coherent conversation, but we never discussed any of the important things, the possibility of her dying, arrangements she might want made for her funeral. Nothing. I so wish now that we had discussed those things. I knew she loved me and I told her that I loved her, but I would also have given anything to have had a conversation that summed up our lives together. I would have loved to hear her last words of advice for me or hear what she truly felt about my successes and failures. But it was not to be. I truly believe there was a sense of denial on her part all the way to the end.

Thirty-six hours before she passed, Mom stopped talking, although I think she knew we were there. Then she developed what we were later told was the "death rattle." It was the sound of fluid filling her lungs, and even though she was comatose and on morphine, Dad was adamant that someone reduce the fluid.

Toby and I found a respiratory therapist who knew Mom was dying but recognized that it would benefit Dad to see Mom helped. She siphoned some of the fluid out of her airway. Even though we knew it would not change anything, Dad seemed a little less overwhelmed.

That last night we were all so exhausted that we took turns staying up with Mom, knowing that the end could come at any moment. Dad and I had fallen asleep during Toby's watch. Toby, too, drifted off while he was holding her hand, and I woke to the sound of Toby saying in a frightened voice, "Mom, Mom!"

Apparently Mom had flinched while he held her hand and he woke up to find her not breathing. There was a gasp for air shortly after Toby shook her hand and by the time Dad and I got to the bedside, Mom was struggling for every slow breath. It was at that point that we all kissed her on the cheek, then I told her it was okay, it was time for her to go. One large tear ran down Mom's face, even though she had not blinked in more than a day.

I fully believe that the flinch Toby felt was Mom's soul leaving her body. It was a touching and spiritual moment, and by far the saddest one of my life. I've been told that other than losing a child, losing your mother is the most difficult thing a person could ever experience.

I looked at the clock and it was 4:24 A.M. on November 2. I also remember it was a Saturday night, the night everyone set their clocks back for daylight savings.

■　■　■

IT TOOK A long time for me to get over the fact that there was nothing I could have done for Mom. I could not heal her, nor find a way for the doctors to help her. I could not find the "magic" potion or course of treatment that would save her life. To this day I hear about new treatments and think, "Wow, that might have worked for Mom."

The loss of a parent, any parent, is profound. It affects you for the rest of your life, and the combination of great memories and what-ifs collide in a roller coaster of emotion that never fully stops. But when a child who was at one time as dependent on a parent as I was loses that parent, it makes the loss that much more painful.

I say this in deference to anyone who has lost a loved one. I do not intend to discount anyone's pain or experience. But the bond I had with my mom that was created by the dressing, bathing, and everything else, going on past my college years, can never be replaced. I think of her often and now, several years after she passed, those thoughts are often about good times. Still, I will miss her profoundly every day for the rest of my life.

19

TAKING LIFE TO
THE NEXT LEVEL

Mom's death released something in me that I'm only now starting to understand. As you have seen, over the years it had become more and more difficult to manage my business holdings, career, and increasingly full personal life. Because of that my drinking and partying with women were getting out of control. The passing of my mom only amplified this behavior and the behavior was now my medication. I was so numb I had to drink to feel any emotion.

One evening in late 2009 or early 2010, my drunkenness caused me some serious bodily harm. At that time John Rich was part owner of a private club downtown called The Spot. I was out on the balcony at The Spot smoking a cigar well after midnight when a female friend Jen called up to me from the street below.

I was well into my Crown and Coke when I went down to

see her, and Jen kneeled down on the sidewalk as we talked. It was late enough that the clubs on Broadway were emptying out and the cabs were filling up. Before too long a guy comes by and starts coming on to Jen. I told him Jen and I were having a conversation and that he should probably move on. He said, "I'm not talking to you." Then he cussed at Jen and walked off with a very negative comment about talking to a midget.

"What the —— did you say?" I called after him as I started rolling toward him. Next thing I knew the guy hit me twice on left side of the head and I was on the ground. Several cab and limo drivers helped me back onto my scooter. When I hit the ground I bit my tongue and blood was everywhere. I had road rash all over my body and a huge black eye.

In my haze I realized that someone had called the police and I made a police report. Then another person brought me a bag of ice. I went right back to partying. Within minutes I had a girl riding around with me on my scooter. It was almost dawn when I drove home and went to bed.

The next day my friends Carolyn Miller and Charlie Pennachio insisted that I go to Vanderbilt Hospital to get my head checked out. X-rays indicated there were no fractures, although the whites of my eyes were completely red. The strangest thing about that entire scene (before, during, and after) was that it did not occur to me at all that I'd had too much to drink.

This was just one example of how after Mom passed I did not take the time to grieve. I'm not sure I knew how. I began seeing a therapist again, and she helped me begin peeling away the layers of my life. For me, it was a sometimes painful process, but together, over the past few years, we've had quite a bit of success.

I also went back on a low-level antidepressant that worked well for me.

One component that I needed to change that I did not deal with or comprehend at this time was my excessive abuse of alcohol. By this time drinking was not about fun and more about self-medicating, and there is never a positive outcome to that scenario. My self-medicating led me into more negative scenarios, which led to more anxiety and shame, which led to more drinking. It was a vicious merry-go-round and I didn't know how to get off of it. Nor did I want to.

Through a lot of reflection I posed a question. What would my ten-year-old self think of my current self from a character and integrity standpoint? I knew without a doubt that young Fred would be terribly disappointed in my recent behaviors. That thought created a lot of motivation, but it took many more months before it sank in.

During this time Dad, Toby, and I filed Chapter 11 bankruptcy and began reorganization. If you have filed for bankruptcy (I hope you haven't, but I know many of you have), then you know the intense sense of defeat and failure, the high levels of stress and anxiety, the feeling of your stomach swirling around so fast inside your body that you just know your entire world is going to crash down on top of you. Ninety percent of my reaction was due to something as simple as pride.

Bankruptcy is a legal tool used as a last resort. While I do not advise going this route if there is any possible other road to take, I was glad it was there for me. An additional problem we had was our less-than-helpful attorney. He was a nice guy, but not as experienced as we would have liked for the complexity of our operation and pending reorganization. Ultimately, after two and a half agonizing years of jumping through hoops the bankruptcy was dismissed. As a company we were no better off than we had been before filing. Once again I took it upon myself and began dealing with each bank directly. One by one I began to resolve our issues.

There was something about being brought to my knees in business that led to my being brought to my knees spiritually. As I have mentioned, ours was a family that thought of church more as an obligation than a gift. Any religious traditions that we observed we did because our parents, grandparents, and great-grandparents had done the same things. There was no real sense of God in any of it.

My business and personal successes and failures, and the deaths of three of my grandparents and my mom, began a deeply rooted change inside of me. On July 1, 2010, I was part of a small group of friends who stayed late after a political event at the home of syndicated radio host, author, speaker, and Financial Peace University founder Dave Ramsey. In addition to Dave and his wife Sharon, a few people who have come to be my closest friends, including country music stars T. G. Sheppard and Kelly Lang, were there.

I had been mulling over life and spirituality in my brain for some time. But due to my structured Catholic upbringing, I was not anywhere close to the top of the list of people you might think were going to be saved. In fact, I was probably in one of the lower percentiles, not because I didn't believe, but because I didn't understand.

Part of my reluctance had to do with my vision of making a lifelong commitment to God and in thinking I had to be in control and do everything on my own. In my mind, to be saved you had to be part of a megachurch and line up in public with a long

line of other sinners so you could be touched on the forehead
by the pastor before you fell dramatically to the ground. If that's
how you got saved, congratulations! My point is that I didn't realize there was any other way.

I am not one to idolize a "rock star" preacher. In fact, the
Bible specifically states that we should not do that and clearly
says we should have no other idol than God. That was something
else I didn't understand. For most of my adult life I had idolized
women, money, fame, sex, alcohol, gambling, and success. But
those are all material things. In the larger scheme of life they
mean nothing. I am amazed that it took me thirty-six years to
figure that out; however, I am also grateful that I figured it out
at all. I still like some of the things I used to idolize. Obviously
money and success are high on that list, but now I realize that
my one true idol is God, and I have Dave, Sharon, T.G., and Kelly
to thank for that. My faith has allowed me to view my struggles
as progress rather than a lack of perfection.

We were all sitting on Dave's back porch that evening when
I began asking him and the others questions about God. I'm not
sure why I chose that moment to start that particular conversation. I hadn't been planning to talk of God that night but the
dialogue took a turn and it seemed the most natural thing in the
world for the discussion to go that direction.

It is no secret that Dave is a spiritual person. He answered
all my questions very astutely, then asked if I'd like to pray the
Sinner's Prayer.

I said, "Yes, but what does that mean?"

Dave told me it meant I would start my life with God over
with the slate wiped clean. All my transgressions would be for-

given, all the times I was selfish instead of giving, all the times I put alcohol above people, all the times I was a disappointment to others rather than the inspiration I wanted to be. All of that, in God's hands, would be taken away.

I knew I was not only ready for this, I was hungry for it.

We all held hands, and Dave recited the prayer one line at a time. I repeated each line back to the group and he paused before reciting the next line, so the full meaning of each word could sink in.

Heavenly Father, have mercy on me, a sinner.
I believe in you and that your Word is true.
I believe that Jesus Christ is the Son of the living God and that he died on the cross so that I may now have forgiveness for my sins and eternal life.
I know that without you in my heart my life is meaningless.

I believe in my heart that you, Lord God, raised Him from the dead.
Please, Jesus, forgive me for every sin I have ever committed or done in my heart.
Please, Lord Jesus, forgive me and come into my heart as my personal Lord and Savior today.
I need you to be my Father and my friend.
I give you my life and ask you to take full control from this moment on.
I pray this in the name of Jesus Christ.

Amen.

By the time we were finished several people were crying, and while I can definitely say it wasn't a Bible-thumping revival experience, it definitely was a spiritual one, and very real. I'll never forget that Dave also told me that the next day when I woke up that there would not be an instant change in my life. However, the air would smell better and the grass would feel different. For me it was more subtle than that, but my life did change, and continues to do so.

Since then, spiritually, I've learned how much I don't know. I've also learned how much I want to know. I've learned that I am not a big fan of the term "saved." Some people call it "becoming a believer." I'm not a fan of that term either, because this very personal process with God does not need a title.

A lot of people ask what religion I am and that poses an entirely different set of questions. I believe that spirituality and your relationship with our Creator are more important than the specific organized religion you may or may not belong to. I believe that it is an individual choice about what you believe. Many denominations are very close in their theology, but it all comes back to God and what God wants for you in your life.

To make a long story short, I was baptized and confirmed Catholic, and I do not denounce that. However, I consider myself nondenominational, but my faith, understanding, and spirituality continue to grow every single day.

Over the course of the next few months I found some specific ideas that helped me stay true to myself. One of these ideas was to make a list of values that were important to me, such as honesty, trust, respect, determination, friendship, and confidence. I'd then concentrate on one item from the list each week, take it to a new level for me, reflect on it every day, and find quiet time to have meaningful conversation with God about it.

With my values reprioritized, I found that the various areas in my life began to feed off each other in a positive way. One area would give me the challenge I needed to stay focused on the others, and vice versa. It seemed a natural progression for me to start businesses in the entertainment field with the founding of an artist development and management company, as well as a film and television production company. Filmmaking and screenwriting had always been of interest to me and these ventures allowed me to explore (and exploit!) both my business side and my creative juices. Along with this came the beginnings of a career in acting.

I had been involved in these areas of business before I recited the Sinner's Prayer, but none of it really came together until after. Now I continue to be amazed at all the opportunities that come my way—in all aspects of my life. But it took taking a huge step back to find focus and outline my priorities before I could realize what a gift life is.

■　■　■

THERE WAS STILL one area of my life that was left unresolved, and that was my excessive drinking. It took several shameful and catastrophic experiences for me to realize the problem and make the commitment to change.

In late 2010 I attended several holiday parties that were over well before midnight. But my parties lasted well into the next day. All of the parties involved alcohol, mostly beer or wine.

It was at that point that I often got a ride home, then called a cab to go back out by myself, perusing local bars and getting drunker and drunker. On more than one occasion I used the Internet to order paid female company. It was not the first time I had done this, and I became more and more disgusted with myself.

Alcohol and/or rejection was always the reason that influenced my decision to order women from the Internet. And I was always hammered when I called numbers I found on Craigslist. Sometimes I'd call multiple numbers, but I stopped doing that when I realized all of the calls went to the same "madam."

Sometimes when I had cashed a check I'd get two girls. The check, of course, should have gone to pay bills. The first few times I was so drunk I can't even remember what the girls looked like. As a fitting tribute to my debauchery, one time one of the girls even stole my diamond watch that had been given to me as a gift.

The theft of my watch was one thing that finally led me to stop drinking. It was the last few days of 2010 and I had hit rock bottom. Fortunately, it was about this same time that a few good friends pulled me aside to discuss my drinking. I finally understood that excessive drinking in no way fit the objectives I had set for myself in life. So I took constant and active control and on January 1, 2011, I made a personal vow to remain true to someone my ten-year-old self would be proud of. This included removing the consumption of alcohol from my life.

I met Bill Moore at the start of my relationship with the MuzikMafia. He is a former William Morris booking agent who left that company to help administer Mafia business. Over the years Bill and I were cohorts in more debauchery than I could ever have imagined. Although we have great stories, we're both lucky to be alive.

Bill became sober three years before I did and was an extremely important part of my decision to quit drinking. After a few failed attempts, when he realized I was serious, he agreed to come over to my apartment to help me get rid of all of the alcohol I had left.

I never drank in my apartment—I was always more of a social drinker—but I had a nice supply of alcohol tucked away in various places for when friends came over. Most was out of my reach, but there was a jar of moonshine in my refrigerator. Bill was running late and I was determined to get rid of the moonshine by dumping it in the toilet, but for the life of me I could not get the jar open. I was determined not to be deterred, so I got a big plastic tub, put the jar in the tub, and pulled out a five-pound sledgehammer. It took me ten powerful swings, but I smashed that jar to smithereens. It was as empowering as anything I'd ever done.

Next I pulled all the beer out of the fridge. I had bought a twelve-pack of cans of Pabst Blue Ribbon the day I moved in five years ago and still had one left. Before Bill arrived I drank the entire can of PBR in one sitting as my official last drink. I then took the sledgehammer and smashed the living daylights out of the can, leaving it flattened. About that time Bill arrived and we poured out numerous bottles of liquor.

I also had a case of loose Corona bottles wedged in sideways at the top of the fridge. Because Corona bottles are clear, every time I opened the door the light in the refrigerator cast a hazy glow over the bottles. But after the bottles were removed, all I saw inside the refrigerator was a clear, white light.

I could not reach the sink to dump the Corona down the drain, so I threw the beer bottles into the tub with the smashed jar of moonshine. One bottle after the other, I reached inside myself and pulled out all the rage and anger and disappointment alcohol had caused me. I threw each bottle as hard as I possibly could and every single bottle shattered with a resounding and satisfying crash.

■ ■ ■

IN RETROSPECT, THE only fix was to take alcohol completely out of my life. I initially made the commitment to stop drinking for one year, but my newfound sobriety has brought me so much clarity that I have decided that alcohol does not need to be part of my life at all. Now that I am sober, I get a legitimate massage when I need touch. It's healthy for me, and it is enough. I am also dating here and there, and because I am sober I remember the touches from my women friends and find I no longer crave touches from paid "escorts." I have also come to realize that I am the kind of person who, after the second drink or so, cannot stop. When I was drinking, as time went on, my "off" button became harder and harder to reach.

Bill introduced me to the book *Power to Choose: Twelve Steps to Wholeness* by Mike O'Neil. The idea behind the book is that you can choose what has power over you. I chose God and made a conscious decision that none of my previous obsessions would ever have that kind of power over me again.

I began working the steps in the book in January 2011 and it has been an invigorating experience, to say the least. Think counseling on steroids. One thing it made me realize was that I was thirty-six years old. It was time to grow up. I had been in the entertainment business for seven years. Alcohol began as a component of my life, and it ended up that my life became a component of it. "It" being the "party" in which I had been quickly losing myself. Where was I?

One of my big fears in giving up alcohol was that my friends would denounce me for it. There is a lot of partying that goes on in the entertainment business and I didn't want anyone to think that all of a sudden I would put a damper on their fun. But everyone, and I mean *everyone,* has been much more accepting and supportive than I ever thought they would be.

I also thought I'd have trouble with other people accepting my story, my testimony, but that was not the case either. In January 2011 I went on a weekend men's retreat. It was held by the church I now attend, The Village Chapel. There, I told sixty-five men, most of whom I had never met before, my story with alcohol and also with paid sex. Giving my testimony was incredibly empowering. It was like pulling scabs off my soul. All the men there were supportive and with each passing day I felt stronger and surer of my commitment to take a different path.

I worked the twelve steps in order but had a lot of anxiety about the fifth step. The fourth step is where you take a written inventory of anything and everything you have done to hurt someone else or yourself in life. The fifth step is where you tell another human being everything that is on that list. These were things I had never, ever said out loud to anyone before. The person you are telling must also have done the fifth step themselves.

I didn't sleep at all the night after I did that. I kept thinking of things I unintentionally forgot to mention, and I felt raw, with my emotions falling all over the place. That said, I also was energized by the experience and began thinking of all the things I needed to do to with my new life. I was also energized by the experience as all the things I could now do began flowing in.

I can now see that I was more than ready for this rebirth. What has helped tremendously is that so many people, after I have shared my story, have said, "You did that too?" Those words have made me feel so much less alone, made me feel like I am no different from anyone else who has made this choice. I have to say that my community of recovery is a very positive one.

Through the steps, the one thread that kept coming up over and over in my testimony is that of abandonment. I felt abandoned when Mom died, when my grandparents passed, when my businesses failed, when girls I liked just wanted to be friends. Over and over abandonment was a recurring theme in my life.

On the flip side, I began to wonder why I have such a need for, and issue with, control. I realized in addition to my physical stature there were many years in my life when I had no control over anything other than my thoughts. This led the way for alcohol and my other obsessions to control me and drain me mentally, emotionally, and physically.

As part of the steps I decided to write down all the good in my life and all of the bad and break it down into the ages and stages of my life. Then I talked with each person who had helped make that time either good or bad. That was an emotional, but freeing, process.

Then I made a "grateful" list and was amazed at all the many things I am grateful for. If you have never done this, it's a wonderful exercise that helps put life in perspective. I also read through all the steps, and read a lot of Scripture, more in six months than I had in my entire life. But most importantly, I began spending regular quiet time with God and found a peace I had never known before. Jesus truly is the Prince of Peace.

MY ONGOING
ADVENTURES

As you've read, I've learned a lot in my first thirty-six years. And most of what I've learned is the product of my own making and failures. The biggest lesson I've learned is to keep everything in perspective, because perception definitely is reality. If you think about it, how others perceive us, and how we perceive others and situations, determines our every motive and reaction. It's a deep thought and it took me a while to get to it. Once I did, it changed my life for the better.

Something else I've learned is that, in my opinion, education is at least 80 percent learning the process of learning and 20 percent the content of learning. I believe this is especially true in college. Not many retain the majority of the content we are taught, but that doesn't matter. What is important is learning *how* to learn and how to find information that is important to you. If you master the process of learning, the world really can be at your fingertips.

I believe and have read many times over that without a doubt the only way to truly learn something is to fail at it. Within every failure there can be a positive learning experience. It took me a long time to understand that concept. Hopefully you will learn more quickly than I did. So hurry up and fail.

Once you do—and you will—perseverance is the only antidote. You have to pick yourself up off the ground (or in my case, get out from under the desk) and find another path that will get you where you need to go. I have found the more failures the better, because the more often you fail, the more you learn. In time you will have one big success that will blow all the other, smaller failures out of the water. So think smart, analyze, learn, find a mentor, persevere.

Dr. Kuratko was, and still is, my mentor, but I had another man strongly influence me, even though he probably never knew it. In 1999 I sent a certified letter to Donald Trump asking for a meeting. I wanted to discuss my business troubles with him to see if he had any ideas that might help me avoid failure. I promptly got a letter back from his personal assistant, Margaret. That letter politely stated that Mr. Trump did not have time to meet with me. But Mr. Trump wanted me to know that perseverance is everything and not to give up. As you have seen, I took that advice to heart.

In another full circle, in 2011 I appeared several times on Mr. Trump's reality show, *The Celebrity Apprentice,* when John Rich was a contestant. That was another surreal experience for me.

All of us in John's inner circle were thrilled to hear that John was going to be on the show. I was especially excited because I strongly support his charity, St. Jude Children's Research Hospital. As a child who was in the hospital a lot, I know what great work they do at St. Jude's.

One of John Rich's best traits is that he is the most loyal person I have ever met in my life. Period. He also has the ability to plug people into places in his life where they fit best and can flourish on their own—such as he did for Cowboy Troy, Gretchen Wilson, and me. I have rarely asked John for anything. Anything he has done for me, or for others, he did because he chose to. Through the years I have learned that those kinds of people don't come along too often.

That's why when I learned when John was going to be taping, I was on call. I knew if John had the opportunity to involve Troy, or me, or anyone else, he would. Sure enough, the call came and the next thing I knew I was on a plane to New York City.

I was overwhelmingly excited about this opportunity, and not only because I wanted to do what I could to represent John and the city of Nashville well. I was also excited because seven years earlier, just after we had taped the "Save a Horse (Ride a Cowboy)" video, I had sent in an application to be a competitor on the very first season of *The Apprentice*. I wasn't chosen then, but for me it felt like I was coming full circle with this appearance on *The Celebrity Apprentice*.

The first trip was a quick there-and-back. A group of us from Nashville went up and I think the segment producer was thrilled to see us come off the plane, because between John's bodyguard Six (Brandon Glasgow), who is six foot nine and covered in tattoos; one of John's artist development partners (Charlie Pennachio), who is about five foot four with long straight black hair down his back; a representative from the charitable division of

Dollar General (Denine Torr), a pregnant professional woman; and myself, we were as diverse a group of people you could get.

The task that day involved creating art and selling it at an art show. I think our Nashville posse added a lot a lot of flair to the episode, and the producers must have thought so, too, because they did not balk when John said he wanted to bring us back for the next episode, in which his team had to create an advertising campaign for a sunscreen called Australian Gold.

John's team, Backbone, had the idea to do a pirate theme and this time when I got the call I was told to find all the pirate garb I could find and be prepared to stay in New York for three days. Fortunately, Nashville has a studio-quality costume shop and they were able to take care of me. In another stroke of luck, this was the day after Halloween and a Monday. Normally the costume shop was not open Mondays but because of the recent Halloween holiday they had made an exception. No coincidences here!

This trip I got to spend more time with some of the other contestants. I already knew Lil Jon and had met Gary Busey at Larry the Cable Guy's Comedy Central Roast a few years back, so it was great to catch up with them. And Mark McGrath and Meat Loaf could not have been nicer. I'd met Richard Hatch on the first trip, but he had been "fired" before I returned.

Like so many people in this country I watched each episode with bated breath. I was thrilled when John became one of the final two contestants, along with Marlee Matlin. Of course, I hoped that John would win, but as far as I was concerned, after twenty-seven hours on primetime national television, with both contestants raising over a million dollars for their charities, everyone won.

For the live finale I flew on a private jet along with Dave Ramsey; his wife, Sharon; and Kelly Lang, whose husband, T. G. Sheppard, had a show booked and could not attend. When we got to New York we met up with a few more friends: country legend Larry Gatlin and our U.S. congresswoman from Tennessee, Marsha Blackburn. Ronnie Barrett, the inventor and manufacturer of the Barrett .50 caliber sniper rifle used by the United States military, was also there, along with his wife. To say we were truly a motley crew is an understatement.

After we all had lunch with John and his wife, Joan, I became engulfed with anxiety and excitement. I so much wanted John to win that my stomach was doing flip-flops. John went back to take a nap and I remember wondering how he could do that. I wasn't even a contestant and there was absolutely no way I could even close my eyes that afternoon.

After dinner, where we had some interesting conversation, Larry Gatlin unofficially became my "handler." He helped me find elevators and exits and at one point, when I was walking, made sure other people did not step on me, which can be an issue. I wanted to pinch myself to be sure this was really happening. The legendary Larry Gatlin was acting like my tour manager! Larry is a great guy, and I will remember him forever for his kindness that day.

Before the show began we were all able to go backstage, and I was surprised at how laid-back it was, considering they were going live in a few minutes. The time I spent sitting in my seat was the longest two hours of my life. I can't imagine how John and Marlee got through it. When Trump finally announced John as the winner, Marc Oswald, John's manager, who was sitting beside me, helped me stand up in my seat so I could see and cheer with the rest of the crowd.

I wasn't just cheering John's win, I was cheering the success of someone who had worked hard his entire career, whose loyalty to his friends is unparalleled, who had not so long ago been a starving artist. John's story is every man's story and gives me hope that every one of you reading this book can also achieve the success you dream of, as John has done.

At the after-party Marlee was as gracious as I knew John would have been had he not won. I also met a lot of people there, including Ivanka Trump, who is as tall as she is beautiful. And when I say tall, think of it from my three-foot-two perspective. In heels she is close to her dad's six foot three.

I was one of the last to leave the after-party and as I scootered out the door stone-cold sober I thought back to my first entertainment-world after-party, just a little more than seven years before. Never in a million years would I have imagined the peaks and valleys my life has taken me through. I am blessed to have met many of our country's top political leaders, sports stars, actors, entertainers, and others whom I could never have dreamed of meeting, much less becoming friends with. It was time to pinch myself again. But it was more real than ever, and it continues to be.

■　■　■

ALTHOUGH I HAVE made every effort to continue to better my life and the lives of others, I have not always been successful. When I went to a large music industry event in spring of 2011,

I am sorry to say that I had a drink. I broke close to one hundred days of not having any alcohol and I can clearly state that it was totally and absolutely not worth it. I was trying to impress a girl and in the middle of my efforts I found that old habits die very hard. It was in the wee hours of the morning and the girl ordered the drink for me without asking what I wanted. I have since realized the girl would probably have been no more or less impressed if I had changed the order to something nonalcoholic. Today, I'm very proud of myself for stopping at that one drink, which I did.

Right now my only vices are cigars and caffeine. Abraham Lincoln once said, "Show me a man without vice, and I will show you a man without virtue." Taking one day at a time, I do look forward to a day when the only stimulation I need is thoughtful prayer.

I am also making a serious effort to eat more healthily. This is something I went years without doing, but as I grow older I realize more and more the importance of what you put in your body. I know for me that good food and the right combination of vitamins makes me feel great, and when I feel great, I am able to take on the world. Bring it on.

I still have not met the woman I want to spend the rest of my life with, but I have renewed efforts to find her. There is a real difference between going out with someone from the standpoint of lust and going out with a woman who might someday be the mother of your children. As much as I had wanted to be in a relationship in years past, I can see now that I was nowhere near ready for that kind of commitment and responsibility. But I know my soul mate is out there and due to my faith I am no longer obsessed with finding her, only hopeful, because I know God will lead us to each other when the time is right.

I also am pleased that I finally have a platform from which I can give back to others. It took me a long time to understand that before I could receive, I had to be intentional about giving. I had to tear down my walls to be able to receive all the good things God sent my way.

Life is an amazing journey and each of us travels our own path. I am so grateful that you chose to spend part of your journey reading this book. Maybe my story will help you choose a different path or strengthen your walk on the path you are on.

If I have learned one thing it is that we are all connected. We are all God's children, and we all have the ability to make a difference in the lives of others. I am pleased that through this book I have connected with you. I have a lot more life to live and hope I will have the privilege of meeting you in person someday. Until then, may you walk in God's grace and have a little fun along the way.

AFTERWORD

BY JOHN RICH

Fred and I became friends several years before Big & Rich was a reality. At first, his physical stature intrigued me. You just don't see people who look like Fred every day. Then when we talked, I realized his charisma was over the top. There was truly something special in this man. The first time we ever hung out was in a honky-tonk on Lower Broad in Nashville. I was onstage jamming and Fred was in the crowd rousing everyone up. That impressed me. How people responded to him impressed me even more.

Since then, I have gotten down on the floor with Fred at several very crowded places, because I wanted to get an inkling of what he sees. I wanted to see the world through Fred's eyes. When you get down there it is a very different world. It is a scary, menacing world full of potential hazards, not the least being stepped on or knocked over or having something fall on you. If you can imagine yourself in a forest and never being able to see the tops of the trees, that is what Fred lives with every day.

Also, to communicate well with anyone you have to be able to look a person in the eye. Fred does not always have that privilege, because even when he is on his scooter most people are so much taller. That's why his story is all the more powerful, because Fred has made inroads to people and places in the world of country music and beyond that no one gets to. No one has all the connections that Fred has and that says volumes about who he is as a person. I continue to be amazed by and respectful of all that Fred has accomplished.

I wanted Fred to be part of the "Save a Horse (Ride a Cowboy)" music video because Big & Rich is about showing the world that country music is without boundaries. Fred is a person who easily could live a life full of boundaries, yet he chooses not to. I can't imagine all that he goes through every day, yet he does not think of himself as disabled. In fact, he is one of the most independent people I have ever met and in no way considers his stature a hindrance.

God created Fred a diastrophic dwarf, and if you know the analogy about lemons and lemonade, Fred is the quintessential lemonade maker. One day I asked Fred if he ever wished he was six feet tall and he said no. I asked why and he told me that then he wouldn't be Two Foot Fred; he wouldn't be the person that he is today.

Fred's story is one of inspiration, determination, and perseverance. I admire Fred more than I can say, and now that you know more about his story I hope that you admire him, too.

John Rich
June 2011

ACKNOWLEDGMENTS

FRED GILL:

Before renewing my relationship with Him, God, I almost always balked at the "Bible-thumping," award-winning celebrity who thanked God and Jesus first and foremost in their acceptance speech. What fake people, I thought. Now that I truly have begun communicating with God, I understand their commitment to thank Him, our Creator, before anyone or anything else. I now understand that the Lord, my God, is responsible for creating the universe we all live in, and in my personal life, for creating me along with the wonderful people and situations in my life. With that said, I would like to give praise and a thank-you to Jesus Christ.

A huge thank you to Mom, Dad, Toby, G&G Wilson, G&G Gill, Aunt Linda, Uncle Rick, "The Girls" (Teresa, Jennifer, and Laura), Tom and Darlene Cooley, Scott Dezarn, Brian Lee, Travis Trueblood, Kevin Pollert, David McKain, Angie (Champ) Fletcher,

John Rich, (Big) Kenny Alphin, Cory Gierman, Bill Moore, Dave & Sharon Ramsey, TG and Kelly Sheppard, Jules Wortman, Marc Oswald, Greg Oswald & WMEE, Kathy Armistead, Carey Nelson Burch, Kix Brooks, Marty McIntosh, Earl Brown, David Bennet, Mark Dennis, Jeff Rocker, and Brad and Brett Warren.

Thank you also to the tour managers who put up with me over the past seven years: Shawn Pennington, Steve Schweidel, Tony Stephens, and especially Crystal Dishmon, who treated me like a superstar when she didn't have to. A big round of thanks, too, to all the band and crew members who went above and beyond to make touring work for me, especially Moses, Castro, and Andy for always being there to lift me into or onto one of our wildly unique stage props. Special appreciation goes to Curt Jenkins, who in my mind is one of the best production managers in the business and will no doubt continue that excellence.

I so appreciate all of the artists who have humbly allowed me the opportunity to appear on their stage as an opening act with Big & Rich or as a special guest including, and certainly not limited to, Larry the Cable Guy, Rascal Flatts, Avenged Seven Fold, Gretchen Wilson, The Zac Brown Band, Kenny Chesney, Bon Jovi, Kix Brooks & Ronnie Dunn (Brooks & Dunn), and most importantly, Tim McGraw for allowing me to open his tour, by introducing the Warren Brothers, and obviously Big & Rich!

To all of the music industry veterans who have taken and continue to take power lunches or coffee with me including, but certainly not limited to, Joe Galante, John Esposito, Craig Campbell, Dan Huff, Tommy Baldrica, and Victoria Shaw.

I appreciate the Academy or Country Music and the Country

Music Association for not only accepting, but embracing, such a nontraditional member such as myself. Our industry is lucky to have two of the best organizations in the world to represent us.

Of course, an enormous thank-you also goes to my coauthor, Lisa Wysocky; my agent, Sharlene Martin; and the wonderful group of people at Howard Books. Without them, this book would not be what it is.

My dad served proudly in the United States Army. Last but certainly not in the very least, I'd like to thank all of the men and women who are currently serving, have served, and will serve in our armed forces for the greatest sovereignty in the history if civilization, set forth by Divine Providence, the United States of America!

LISA WYSOCKY:

Thank you first of all to Fred Gill, who is a fabulous writing partner. I so appreciate his candor and honesty in bringing his story to you. I hope you learn even half as much from Fred as I have. He is truly an amazing person . . . and he really does know everybody.

Thanks also to Sharlene Martin at Martin Literary Management, super-agent extraordinaire! She always finds a way to make the deal work and, in addition, is a dear friend whom I value greatly. Kudos must also go to the entire team at Howard Books, who made the process easy and fun. My sincere appreciation to Fido's, and to Starbucks in Green Hills (two of Nashville's best coffee shops), Metro Nashville Parks, and Blackstone Brewpub and Brewery, home of Nashville's best salads and pizzas. Fred and I spent most of our collaborative hours in those places and I am grateful for all of them.

To Fred's family and friends, thank you so much for sharing. The book would not be nearly what it is without you. And finally to you, the reader: thank you for picking up the book. Thank you for reading. If you enjoyed Fred's story, if he inspires you, please recommend the book to others so they too can find encouragement from his life.